The Mathematics Curriculum

FROM GRAPHS
TO CALCULUS

The Mathematics Curriculum: A Critical Review
was a project set up by the Schools Council at the University of Nottingham 1973–77

Members of the central project team were

Professor J. V. Armitage (Principal, College of St. Hild and
St. Bede, Durham), Director
Professor H. Halberstam (Department of Mathematics,
University of Nottingham), Co-Director (1975–77)
Mr. G. R. H. Boys (1973–76)
Mrs. J. A. Gadsden
Dr. R. B. Coates (1973–74)

The books in this series are

Geometry
From Graphs to Calculus
Mathematics across the Curriculum
Number
Algebra
Counting and Configurations
Mathematics in the World
Eleven to Thirteen

The Mathematics Curriculum

FROM GRAPHS TO CALCULUS

Written for the Project by
HILARY SHUARD and **HUGH NEILL**

Published for the Schools Council by BLACKIE

ISBN 0 216 90341 6

First published 1977

Illustrator: Julie Gadsden

Published by Blackie and Son Limited, Bishopbriggs, Glasgow
and 450/452 Edgware Road, London W2 1EG

Printed in Great Britain by Thomson Litho Ltd., East Kilbride, Scotland

Preface

This book is one of a series produced by the Schools Council Project: *The Mathematics Curriculum—A Critical Review*. This Project was initiated by the Mathematics Committee of the Schools Council as a result of letters received from teachers asking for guidance on the vast amount of new mathematical literature which had been produced for schools during the 1960s. The Project was set up in 1973 and was based at the Shell Centre for Mathematical Education at Nottingham University.

It was felt that teachers, who faced a daunting array of mathematical literature and novel classroom material, would welcome a basis for constructive and critical discussion of the content of the school mathematics curriculum. Moreover, whilst the choice of syllabus, books, materials, methods and presentation belonged properly to the teacher, the range of choices was so vast as to make well-informed decisions consistent with professional integrity well nigh impossible; so that any advice implicit in these books, far from detracting from the teachers' role, would rather establish it.

The fundamental aim of the Project, therefore, is to help teachers to perform their own critical appraisal of existing mathematics syllabuses and teaching apparatus for secondary school pupils in the 11 to 16 age range, with the objective of making, for them, optimal choices. Such an aim, however fundamental it may be, is still inadequate. It was never the intention of those responsible for the Project that they should provide only a review of mathematical literature and apparatus, for an exercise of that kind would be obsolescent before the material could be published. Instead, the Project was conceived as a contribution both to initial and to post-experience in-service training, as well as providing helpful private reading.

Although the Project was not intended to be an exercise in curriculum development, it was almost inevitable and certainly desirable that a review of existing syllabuses should lead to a consideration of the possibility of a synthesis of "modern" and "traditional". I believe that such a synthesis is possible and, indeed, sorely needed. So, although we have not attempted to spell out an optimum syllabus, we have tried to identify the important ideas and skills which should be represented at school, and to show how so-called modern and traditional topics are related. We hope that one of the lessons which emerges from these books is that the two can be integrated in a unified presentation of mathematics and its applications. Perhaps the current numeracy debate will lead to syllabus revision. If so, it must be informed by the sound mathematical and pedagogical considerations to which end these books are devoted.

In order to focus as wide a range of experience as possible on the task, planning teams were established, each under the chairmanship of a potential author (an Editorial Fellow) and comprising representatives from Universities, Polytechnics, Colleges of Education, Schools, the Inspectorate and the Advisory Services. The material produced was referred to working groups of teachers across the country—from Cornwall and the Channel Islands to Northumberland. Moreover, the groups were invited to make original contributions as well as to comment on planning material. All the material thus made available was then referred once more to the original planning team, who now assume responsibility for advising the Editorial Fellow on the "final" write-up, which in some cases received further redaction by other writers. The result is now before the reader.

It may seem strange that a book which includes the word "calculus" in its title should appear in a series written about the mathematics curriculum for 11 to 16 year olds. However, although the beginnings of formal calculus are the end-point of this book, the authors believe that ideas such as measurement of area and the concept of a limit should be encountered by every pupil, whether or not he goes on to use these in differentiation and integration.

Further, every school leaver should be able to extract and understand the information contained in the simpler forms of graph. More and more facts are being presented in this way by industry and government, and it is vital that people should have formed the habit of looking critically at suggested interpretations of the data. This is an important prerequisite for a responsible society.

J. V. Armitage

Acknowledgements

The authors wish to thank the many people who have in various ways contributed to the production of this book. Its design and outlook were greatly influenced by the planning team, whose meetings were both thought-provoking and fun. The authors hope that the team's fresh approach to what at first seemed well-worn mathematical paths is reflected in the book. The members of the team were:

Dr. J. A. Anderson, Department of Mathematics, University of Nottingham

Mr. T. Farrell, Sarah Metcalfe Secondary School, Middlesbrough

Mr. A. Gorringe, Chosen Hill School, Churchdown, Nr. Gloucester

Mr. D. S. Hale, H.M.I.

Mr. M. W. Pedelty, South Hackney Secondary School, London

Professor R. L. E. Schwarzenberger, Department of Mathematics, University of Warwick

Mr. E. B. C. Thornton, Claremont Teachers' College, Perth, Australia

They received perceptive comments on, and constructive criticism of, the planning material from Mr. J. K. Backhouse, Dr. T. J. Fletcher and from working groups of teachers in North and South London.

They would also like to thank Mrs. J. A. Gadsden, who has prepared an endless succession of typescripts, together with all the diagrams, and has helped the authors in countless other ways.

Lastly, the authors would like to acknowledge with gratitude permission to reproduce material from:

The School Mathematics Project, Books A to H, and *X to Z*, Cambridge University Press, 1968 to 1974

The School Mathematics Project, Books 1 to 5. Cambridge University Press, 1965 to 1969, and Metric Edition, 1969 to 1971

The Scottish Mathematics Group, *Modern Mathematics for Schools, Books 1 to 9*, Second Edition, Blackie and Chambers, 1971 to 1975

C. V. Durell, *Certificate Mathematics, Volumes 1 to 4*, Bell, 1974 to 1975

Nuffield Mathematics Project: Pictorial Representation, Graphs Leading to Algebra, Chambers and Murray, 1967

Science 5/13: Structures and Forces, Macdonald Educational, 1972–73

SMP, Revised Advanced Mathematics, Book 1, Cambridge University Press, 1973

Reference has also been made to:

J. B. Channon, A. McLeish Smith, H. C. Head, *New General Mathematics, Books 1 to 4*, Longman, 1970 to 1971

D. E. Mansfield, D. Thompson, M. Bruckheimer, *Mathematics: A New Approach*, Chatto & Windus, 1965

Nuffield Physics Teachers' Guide I, Longmans/Penguin, 1966

B. Holland, P. Rees, *Maths Today, Books 1 to 4*, Harrap, 1975

Contents

Introduction

This book is about graphs, their drawing, their interpretation, their development and their use. It discusses the teaching of graphs from their early introduction in secondary schools as far as the beginnings of integral and differential calculus.

Graphs are used in order to convey in a simple pictorial and immediate way ideas which otherwise would require many words, figures or symbols to portray. "Every picture tells a story" is a particularly apt saying in this context; in fact, to those who understand the message, the graphical picture avoids the need for the story by saying it all.

In order to extract as much as possible from graphical messages, pupils must learn to read the messages and to become fluent in the vocabulary of graphical language. Some pupils will learn to read these messages more quickly than others, and these more-able students will progress to the stage where they appreciate the significance of area and gradient; they can then go on to study integration and differentiation. Other pupils who are not so adept at the language will not progress much further than reading and understanding block graphs. All pupils, whatever their ability, should learn to read as many of the messages contained in graphs as they can, for otherwise they will be deprived of a means of communication of proven use.

It is interesting to observe the differences of opinion between teachers of mathematics about the depth of study of graphs which is appropriate for pupils of various abilities. Some GCE "O" Level syllabuses recognize that the concepts of area and gradient are closely associated with graphs, and require that integration and differentiation should be taken as far as obtaining algebraic formulae and their application. Other syllabuses require only approximate calculation of area and gradient. There are still other "O" Level syllabuses which do not include area under a graph or gradient of a curve. CSE syllabuses contain just the same range of views about the extent of graphical work as GCE syllabuses do. The introduction of a common system of examinations at sixteen would, no doubt, produce syllabuses which reflect a similar range of opinion and practice.

Some teachers who argue against teaching integration and differentiation to the more-able pupils before sixteen, do so on the grounds that an introduction to an important topic shortly before an examination may lead to a hurried approach in which a proper understanding takes second place to the learning of rules to answer examination questions. It is unfortunate that the types of question set in a number of GCE and CSE examinations indicate clearly that an expectation of rote learning is usual in this area of work.

Other teachers argue that it is very important that able pupils whose major interests lie outside mathematics, and whose formal mathematical education will end at age sixteen, should see something of the power of calculus. Some of these pupils will, in the sixth form, study quantitative subjects such as economics or biology or geography, where some knowledge of calculus is very useful. Others will eventually take up positions of responsibility in government, industry or commerce, and will need to make decisions on the basis of numerical and graphical information.

The authors of this book take the second view. They believe that a well-developed understanding of mathematics is a national resource. The more numerate the decision makers, the more likely the decisions are to be well informed. It is because government, industry and business often communicate quantifiable ideas by graphs, and because a knowledge of calculus helps citizens to read and understand these graphs, that calculus assumes its position of importance. We cannot, as a nation, afford not to develop this mathematical skill in our pupils.

However, while holding the second view, the authors try to meet the criticisms expressed by those who hold the first view by keeping integration and differentiation firmly embedded in the context of graphs, and by deploring the mere mechanical "learning of rules" which is not based on understanding of the central concepts of area and gradient. The authors hope that those teachers who disagree with their view, and first teach calculus as part of a sixth-form course, will nevertheless find material which is of interest to them.

New developments in the mathematics curriculum have affected the teaching of graphs in various ways. First, there have been considerable changes in the teaching of functions. In many syllabuses, functions are taught much earlier than before, sometimes appearing as special kinds of relations, and often illustrated by types of diagrams other than the traditional Cartesian graph. Another development has been the increased use of approximate methods to calculate areas under graphs and gradients of graphs. This development is a most valuable stepping stone before the introduction of integration and differentiation, thereby reducing the number of new ideas with which the beginner in calculus has to cope at the same time.

Both these developments have meant that textbook writers have incorporated new ideas into their books. The new material on relations and functions has demanded decisions about their relative importance, while the material on area and gradient has required the writers to handle analytical ideas of some delicacy.

A third development is very new indeed. Modern electronic calculators are now so cheap and so easily available that they have opened up the possibility of a greatly increased emphasis on numerical work, particularly in the teaching of limits and integration. These ideas are discussed in some detail in this book. The greater availability of computing facilities also increases the possibility of numerical exploration of these ideas, but no specific reference has been made to computers, as the principles underlying the use of calculators and computers are the same.

The discussion of the teaching of graphs, area and gradient form the major part of this book. There follows an essay by Professor R. L. E. Schwarzenberger of the Mathematics Department, University of Warwick. This essay traces the historical development of integration and differentiation, and relates history to teaching. In addition to contributing to the book, Professor Schwarzenberger has enthusiastically given the authors most valuable help and guidance throughout its preparation.

The authors believe that pupils should build up their knowledge of important ideas over a number of years, treating the ideas in greater depth and using more powerful techniques as their own thinking develops. The two key ideas of the calculus—area and gradient—are treated in this way in this book, and the order of the chapters reflects this development. In the early secondary years the treatment is *graphical* and *pictorial*. Pupils' increasing arithmetical skill enables many areas under curves to be evaluated *numerically* and, as the concept of ratio develops, pupils are able to find gradients numerically. The final stage of abstraction is the generalization to *algebraic* formulae for integrals and derivatives, and the link between integrals and derivatives. By the age of sixteen, the most-able pupils are reaching a level of thinking when they can handle these abstract ideas. For the rather less able, concentration on the details of algebraic manipulation often prevents appreciation of the underlying ideas, and such pupils should postpone algebraic work on area and gradient until later. However, there is a powerful argument in favour of their meeting the ideas of the calculus in graphical and numerical settings which enable them to have a conceptual background for the later introduction of formal calculus, which is now needed in so many sciences and other subjects. Thus, many teachers will not expect their pupils to cover the content of this book by the age of sixteen, but the book goes as far as the fundamental theorem in calculus, a simple version of which provides a suitable staging post for the most-able pupils.

The first five chapters set the scene by discussing graphical work and functions. Two separate themes develop from this: area leading to integration, and gradient leading to differentiation. These themes are developed throughout the book in parallel with developments based on pupils' experiences of distance, time and speed. The chapters on area and integration always precede the corresponding chapters on gradient and differentiation, because the authors believe that area is conceptually simpler than gradient. Chapters 9 and 10 on numbers and limits take their place because they provide essential background to subsequent work. Chapter 6, Some Special Graphs, is at what seems to be the logical place in the development of the book. The actual order and development of chapters 1 to 15 is shown schematically in the diagram in which abbreviated chapter headings are followed by the chapter number.

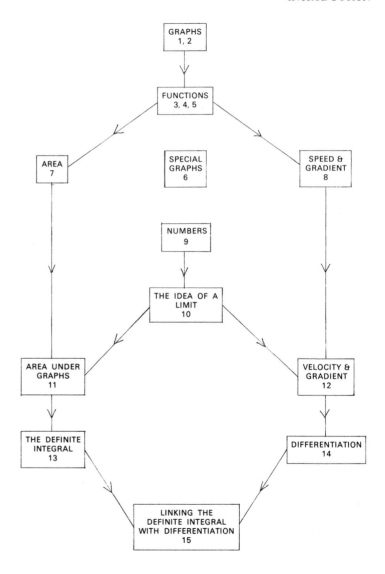

1 The Early Stages of Graphical Work

1.1. Graphical Literacy

Few pupils nowadays reach the age of 11 without having some experience of drawing block graphs; at this stage, however, most children's appreciation of graphical representation is vivid but imprecise. During the years from 11 to 16 they should develop a much greater understanding of how information can be conveyed by Cartesian graphs, and a knowledge of the fact that some information cannot be represented in this way. Their early experience should also help pupils to acquire, through informal examples, an idea of the essential characteristics of *functions*. Pupils should also come to link together the Cartesian graph and other pictures of a function with algebraic representations such as formulae. Graphs are often used to convey information about functions in a vigorous immediate way, but a graph will only get its message across to a person who has learnt to read that message. The growth of graphical literacy, both in the reading of graphs and in the interpretation of their messages, should be one of the main aims of graphical work for all pupils.

The more-able pupils will be able to draw graphs and to make deductions from them, and also to interpret graphs and to make conjectures about the formulae associated with them. Graphs are used to convey information and to assist in the analysing of information. Graphical representation is one of the most valuable mathematical tools used by scientists, economists, government, industry and commerce. Indeed, many pupils will find a variety of uses for graphs in their activities outside mathematics. For less-able pupils the aim of graphical literacy will inevitably be restricted to more limited circumstances, but all pupils can and should have some literacy in graphical work, for the citizen who cannot read a graph is a handicapped member of society.

1.2. Beginnings

We start by looking at some typical examples of graphs drawn by children before the age of 11. These examples draw our attention to several conceptual developments which children need to make in their graphical work. The examples are drawn from the *Teacher's Guides* (*Pictorial Representation* and *Graphs Leading to Algebra*) to the *Nuffield Mathematics Project*; among the children who enter secondary schools will be found some who are capable of drawing each type of graph illustrated. However, the representation most commonly used in primary schools is that of block graphs, and a number of children will have had no other experience of drawing graphs.

Seven-year-old Richard has drawn his graph (figure 1.1) so that each square of the graph represents a child. Whole squares are coloured, and it is natural for Richard to write the numbers of children represented in the centres of the intervals on the axes. The idea that a square of the graph paper represents a unit of a quantity leads naturally to the drawing of histograms. We shall also want a square of graph paper, which is a unit of area, to represent a unit of some quantity such as distance at a later stage (see chapter 11). However, in order to draw a Cartesian graph, Richard needs to supplement his idea of representing numbers by squares with the idea that an axis of a graph is a number-line, so that a point on the axis represents a number, instead of a square of the paper representing a number. Carol, who drew the graph in figure 1.2,

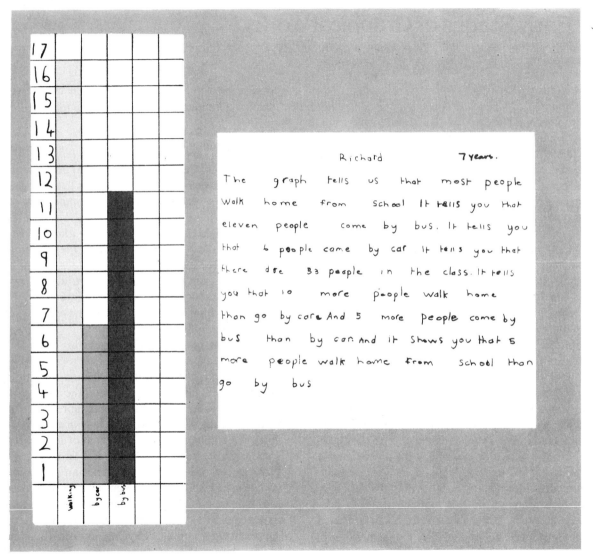

Figure 1.1   From *Pictorial Representation*

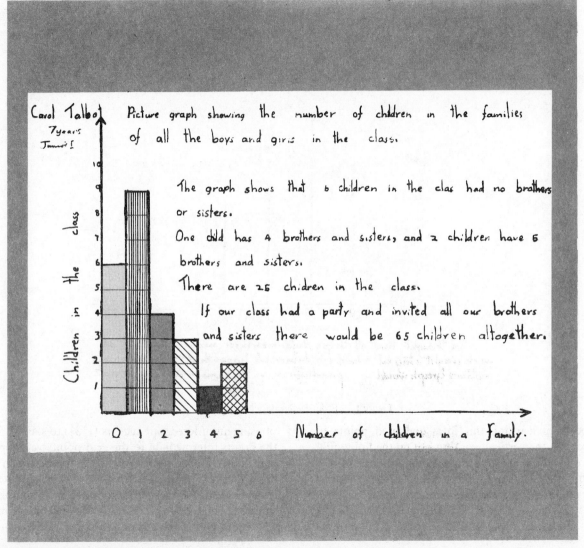

Figure 1.2   From *Pictorial Representation.*

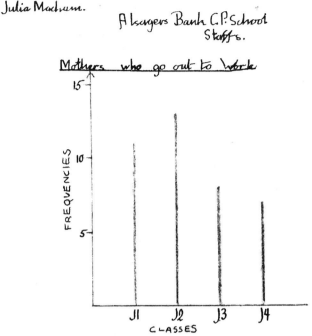

Julia Macham.

A lsagers Bank C.P. School
Staffs.

Mothers who go out to Work

We thought that all those children whose mothers were out at work might stay at school for dinner. We hoped that the dinner and mothers' graph would go up and down in the same order. They do not.

Figure 1.3   From *Pictorial Representation*.

was in the process of learning this idea, and used points to represent numbers on the vertical axis, but not on the horizontal axis. Julia (figure 1.3) was able to draw a line graph instead of a block graph. This stage leads naturally to the Cartesian graphs drawn by Sandra (figure 1.4). She can represent an ordered pair of numbers such as (2, 3) by a point. Many children of 11 are not as advanced as this. We notice, however, that Sandra has not thought of using an ordered pair such as $(1, 3\frac{1}{2})$ to satisfy $\square + 2\Delta = 8$. Do the points intermediate to the grid points yet represent number-pairs to her? What meaning (if any) does she attach to the lines she has drawn to join up the points on her graphs? We cannot tell from these graphs, but these questions are most important in understanding children's interpretation of graphical representations. They commonly join up points they have drawn on the graph

Sandra A. Bergen.

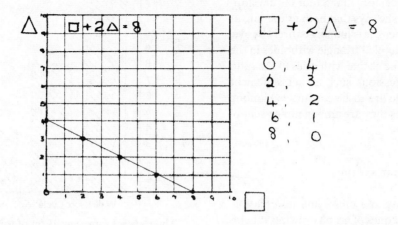

$\square + 2\triangle = 8$

O ,	4
2 ,	3
4 ,	2
6 ,	1
8 ,	0

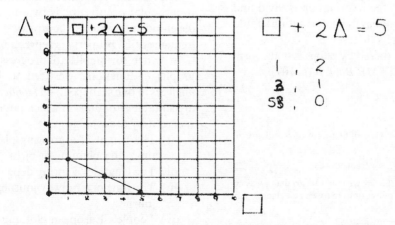

$\square + 2\triangle = 5$

1 ,	2
3 ,	1
5 ,	0

These two graphs are both straight line graphs and are both at the same angle.

Figure 1.4   From *Graphs Leading to Algebra*.

6

merely because they have seen graphs which look like this, although they do not yet understand that all the points of the graph satisfy its equation. We notice, too, that Sandra is developing an intuitive idea of gradient, as she says that both graphs are at the same angle. It is not clear whether she is judging entirely by eye, or whether she knows that a right-angled triangle with sides in the ratio 8:4 is of exactly the same shape as one with sides in the ratio $5:2\frac{1}{2}$. However, spontaneous expressions such as her statement that the lines are at the same angle are to be encouraged among secondary-school pupils as much as they are among junior-school pupils.

1.3. The Introduction of Cartesian Graphs

A graph is a means of recording and conveying information. While pupils are learning the techniques of graph drawing, it helps their understanding considerably if the information is vivid and full of meaning to them. Often, this implies that information should be collected or measured by the pupils themselves.

Much of the information easily gathered by pupils is of the form shown in the quotations below from *SMP Book B* (p. 107).

Here is the result of a survey made on a class of first-form boys and girls to find out how many are using each method:

walk, 13; cycle, 8; bus, 4; train, 9; car, 2.

We can just write the results out like this, or we could try to find a way to display them so that they were easier to follow, or even to see at a glance. The first method suggested is a simple table:

Walk	Cycle	Bus	Train	Car	
13	8	4	9	2	Total 36

The total has been included and this acts as a useful check.

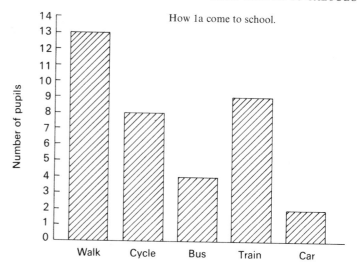

How 1a come to school.

The natural representation of this information, the frequency of a particular occurrence, is by a block graph. This starts a line of development towards the drawing of a *histogram*, in which the frequency of a property is represented by an area.

In order for pupils to progress towards drawing Cartesian graphs of functions, we need to look for situations in which *numbers* in one set depend on *numbers* in another set. The following are suitable situations in which pupils can collect information and record it by drawing graphs:

(i) The height of a growing plant or animal depends on the time after planting or birth.

(ii) The length of a spring depends on the mass hung from it.

(iii) The time of a railway journey depends on the length of the journey.

(iv) People's European clothing size depends on their British clothing size.

(v) The charge for a trunk telephone call depends on the distance.

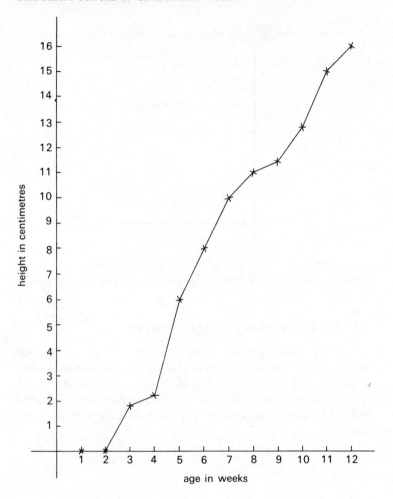

Figure 1.5   The rate of growth of a broad bean shoot.

(vi) The charge for a trunk telephone call depends on the duration of the call.

If pupils are to plot with understanding a point on a graph such as that of the growth of a broad bean plant (figure 1.5), two pieces of knowledge need to be linked together in the representation of the fact that "after 5 weeks, the plant is 6 centimetres high". These are:

   (i) how to plot the point with coordinates $(5, 6)$;

  (ii) the fact that after 5 weeks of growth the plant is 6 cm high is represented by the point $(5, 6)$.

The progression of thought from 5 to 6 is caught by the wording 5 *maps* to 6 and is indicated in some representations by a *mapping arrow*, although in the graph of figure 1.5 the mapping arrow is not seen.

Figure 1.6 shows a possible teaching method. It is important that time is spent on the stages indicated by the first two diagrams.

It may be helpful at this point for the reader to look forward to section 4.2 (page 21).

It is often easier for pupils to read what others have written than to write their own stories; so too they may find it easier to read graphs drawn by other people than to draw their own graphs. They can be helped to imagine the invisible mapping arrows which a graph contains if the teacher asks for sets of ordered pairs to be obtained from a given graph, such as that in figure 1.5:

Fill in the blank in the sentence "The point $(7, \quad)$ lies on the graph".
Where does 7 map to?
Where has 10 come from?
What number maps to 6?

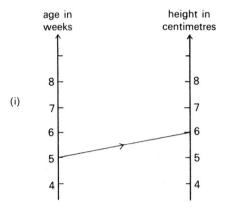

Figure 1.6   (i) The axes of the graph are parallel; the arrow shows that 5 maps to 6.

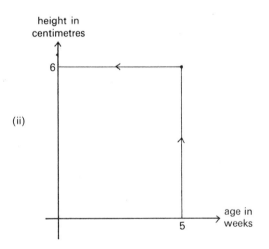

(ii) The axes are perpendicular; the mapping arrow is shown with a right-angled bend in it.

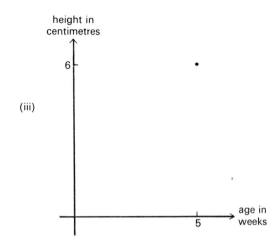

(iii) The mapping arrow is invisible, but the dot marks where it "turns the corner".

1.4. The Expectation of Science Teachers

The quotation opposite from *Science 5/13: Structures and Forces, Stages 1 & 2* (p. 34) is typical of the intuitive understanding of graphs that is often expected of children of age 11 and 12 in science. The topic under discussion is the rate of cooling of a can of hot water when insulated by various materials used in house building.

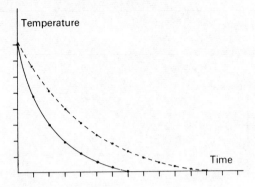

Children may see that 'the steeper the graph, the quicker it is cooling'.

Does the cavity in the walls help to keep the house warm (ie is air a good heat insulator)?

An experiment like the one shown can be tried.

Also typical of the attitudes of science teachers is the quotation below from the *Teachers' Guide I* to *Nuffield Physics* (p. 198). The experiment is that of stretching a spring by hanging weights from it.

> **Graph.** This is a case for plotting a simple graph, if children are ready for it. Children take kindly to graphs provided they are introduced casually, not as something they "should have done in maths", and unfortunately have not.

The authors of this quotation have a very valid point of view. We have seen that most children have drawn many graphs before the age of 11, but in a number of mathematics courses designed for secondary schools this fact is ignored.

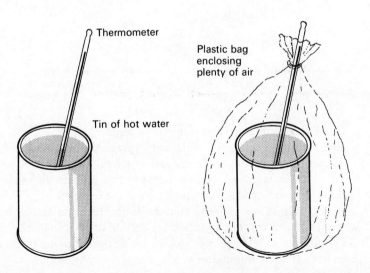

2   Graphs as Mathematical Models

2.1. Graphical Models

We have seen that children of 11 and 12 can use graphs in a very natural way to make a vivid pictorial record of information about numbers and quantities which they have found in the world around them. Graphical representation is, however, more than a *descriptive* tool; its major importance in mathematics is that it is *predictive*. The representation of information in a graph has an immediate visual impact which encourages us to think about the information, to ask ourselves questions, and to draw conclusions.

For instance, we can measure the height of the classroom broad bean plant each Friday afternoon, and draw a dot graph such as that of figure 2.1. This draws attention to one aspect only of the plant's growth: its height. We have ignored its girth, its mass, whether it has grown a new leaf this week, and any other aspects of its behaviour apart from its height.

We have made a *mathematical model* which simulates the particular aspect of the real world in which we are interested; it helps us to focus our attention on the height of the plant to the exclusion of all else, in a way similar to that in which a small boy can concentrate completely on a model car without the noise and danger and uncontrollability of the street scene in real life. He can act out his thoughts in a model world which is completely under his control. Similarly, a mathematical model enables us to concentrate on particular features of the situation, and to act out changes and study their consequences in a way which would be impossible in the real world. The graphical model at this stage is purely descriptive. But the graphical description also suggests questions:

  (i) Does the bean grow steadily?

  (ii) How fast is it growing?

  (iii) How tall should we expect it to be next Friday?

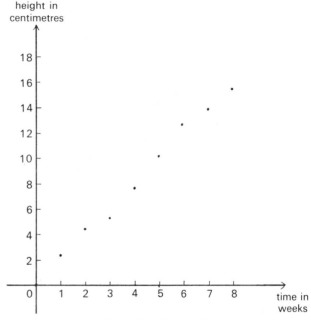

Figure 2.1   First model.

  (iv) Do other plants grow faster or slower?

  (v) Do side shoots grow at the same rate as the main stem?

These questions are questions about plants, but they can be handled within a model, and the answers and predictions made within the model can then be applied back to the real world.

A next step in our thinking may be to improve the model. A straight-line graph is both a simple model and one which displays the continuity of plant growth (which the dot-graph of figure 2.1 does not). It also contains answers to some of our questions.

10

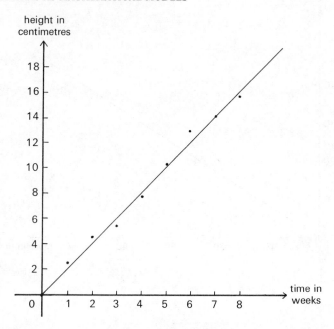

Figure 2.2   Improved model.

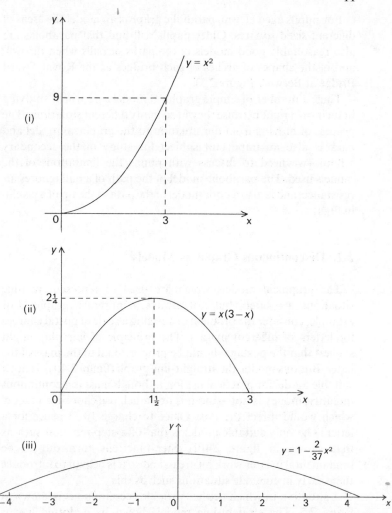

Figure 2.3   Typical parabolic graphs: (i) the areas of squares; (ii) the path of a projectile; (iii) the low arch of the Royal Tweed Bridge, Berwick (after W. W. Sawyer, *Mathematician's Delight*, Penguin).

The straight-line graph represents a rate of growth of about 2 centimetres per week. According to the model, the plant will be approximately 18 cm tall next week. The model has enabled us to predict. Of course, the prediction may not fit real life very well—the plant may die, or reach maturity and stop growing.

It is a feature of our world that a small number of graphical models can be used to fit a great variety of situations fairly well. A straight-line model is a fairly good fit for the velocities at various times of a stone dropped from the hand, for the extensions of an elastic band when pulled with different forces, for the quantities of potatoes needed for different numbers of school dinners, and for many more situations.

For pupils aged eleven, parabolic graphs can model the areas of different-sized squares. Older pupils will find that parabolas are also reasonably good models of the paths of balls when thrown, and of the shapes of arches of such bridges as the Royal Tweed Bridge at Berwick (figure 2.3).

Thus, a number of simple graphical models are worth studying in their own right because they fit so many different situations. The process of moving from the situation to the graphical model and back is also an important subject for study in the secondary school—we need to discuss with pupils the limitations of the models used. The parabolic model of the path of a ball ignores air resistance, and is also a poor model of the path of the tip of a javelin in flight.

2.2. Discontinuous Graphs as Models

The graphical models which are used to represent real-life situations are often, but not always, continuous graphs. For example, consider the problem of devising a scale of postal charges for letters of different masses. The principle of fair play might suggest that the postage should be proportional to the mass of the letter. But this model, the straight-line graph (figure 2.4(i)), is not a suitable model for practical use for, although mass is a continuous quantity, money is not—and it is not much use choosing a model which would direct the Post Office to charge 10·23 pence for a letter. The only suitable model is that of a step-function such as that shown in figure 2.4(ii). Step-functions turn out to be fundamental in later work on areas, and so it is helpful to introduce them early in concrete situations such as this.

A situation in which neither variable is continuous is shown in figure 2.5. The straight-line model shown by a dotted line is illuminating, in spite of the fact that interpolation is useless, there being no shoe sizes between $4\frac{1}{2}$ and 5, for instance.

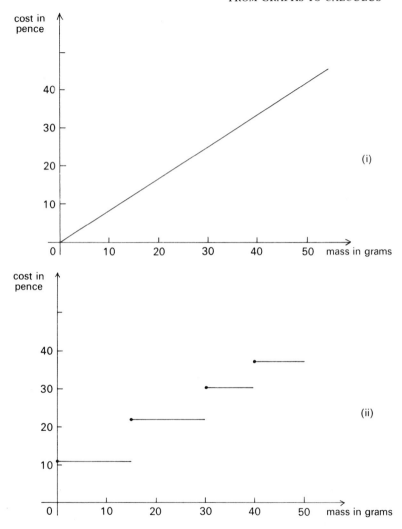

Figure 2.4   Scales of postal charges: (i) an impractical straight-line model; (ii) the step-function used for air-mail letters to America during 1976.

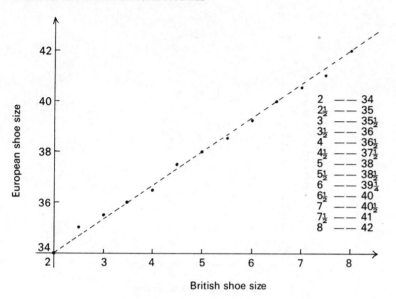

2	34
2½	35
3	35½
3½	36
4	36½
4½	37½
5	38
5½	38½
6	39¼
6½	40
7	40½
7½	41
8	42

Figure 2.5   Conversion graph for women's shoe sizes.

give rise to straight lines and curves, and investigating the properties of these curves, they should not forget that behind their model lies the real world, and that the purpose of what they are doing is to be able to transfer predictions from the models back to the situations which gave rise to them.

2.4. An Example

An example may help to make the development of the modelling process clearer. *SMP Book A* (p. 11) contains the following passage which it uses as a starting point.

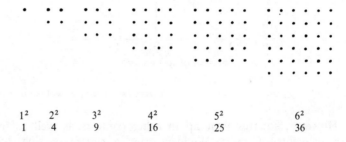

1^2	2^2	3^2	4^2	5^2	6^2
1	4	9	16	25	36

What are the next two numbers of this kind?

Pupils might draw a graph of these square numbers, although the text does not ask them to do so at this stage. Figure 2.6(i) shows a line graph, which many children might draw without much help on entry to the secondary school. During their first year, children should be encouraged to replace the lines of this graph by points, to give the result shown in figure 2.6(ii).

Should the points of this graph by joined up? If so, how?

If the graph is regarded merely as a record of spots arranged in squares, the points of the graph clearly should not be joined up, for we cannot have a square of side 2½ spots.

2.3. Aim of Graphical Work

At the beginning of the secondary school, children think of the graphs they draw as direct records of real situations. A major aim of the work of the years up to 16 is to help pupils to see the graphical model as an entity in its own right, a piece of mathematics which can be studied apart from the situation which gave rise to it. However, this process of abstracting a mathematical model from a real situation can be treated in such a way that pupils do not always realize that it has taken place, so that the model, for instance the straight line or parabola, seems to them to be divorced from reality, and to have no connection with the real situation which it modelled. The teacher needs to be sure that, while pupils are working within the model, that is, studying equations which

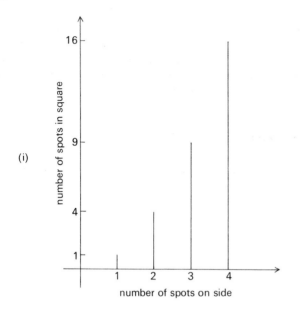

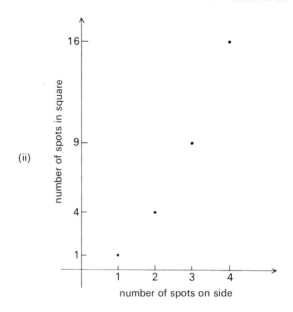

Figure 2.6   The squares of positive whole numbers: (i) line graph; (ii) point graph.

However, squares turn up in other contexts as well as in arrangements of spots. We can draw a square of side 2·5 centimetres, and we can also use the arithmetic process of squaring the number 2·5.

A graph showing the squares of all the real numbers models the squaring of fractional, as well as of whole, numbers. Hence it is more useful, and leads pupils towards a greater knowledge of the real number system. Thus teachers may think it sensible to encourage pupils to join the points in figure 2.6(ii) by drawing a smooth curve through them (figure 2.7), thus setting the graph which was originally concerned with spots within a wider mathematical context.

Later developments of graphical work are discussed in succeed-

ing chapters. However, we should note here that, when directed numbers and their multiplication make an appearance, we shall extend the quadratic or parabolic model which maps the real number x to x^2, and which is usually written either $y = x^2$ or $x \mapsto x^2$, to allow x to be a directed number (figure 2.8). Pupils will also get used to seeing the parabola in a number of different positions, and will eventually see that this model applies to a problem such as:

100 metres of fencing is used to make three sides of a rectangular enclosure against a wall. What is the greatest area which can be enclosed?

Thus we see that a major aim of the work is to give the parabolic model, and the formula $x \mapsto x^2$ for the function, a life of their own

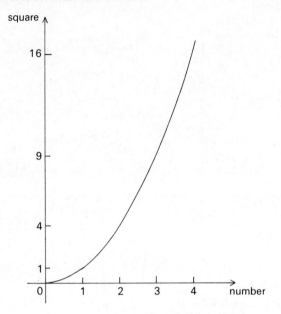

Figure 2.7   The squares of positive real numbers.

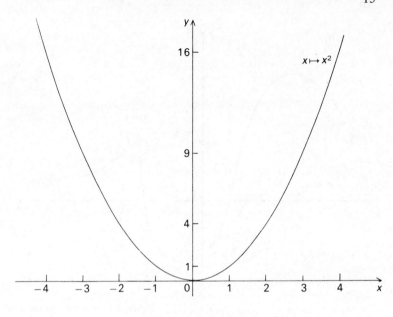

Figure 2.8   Graph of $x \mapsto x^2$.

within the pupil's mind. By the age of 14 or 15, the more-able pupils will be considering problems about the mathematical model and, for instance, the gradient of the graph of $x \mapsto x^2$ can be studied without immediate reference back to the real-life situations being modelled.

2.5. Looking Forward

Among the many graphical models available, there are two types which are particularly useful. These are loosely described as *continuous graphs* and *graphs of step functions* (figure 2.9). In this book, therefore, we shall concentrate particularly on pupils'

development towards, and study of, these two general categories of graphical model. The unifying concept of a *function* is of particular importance in this study, and the next chapter discusses the concept.

2.6. A Recommendation

The early treatment of graphical representation in secondary schools is often disappointing. The location and the plotting of points are usually introduced in the first year, but the subsequent development of graphical work seems to take two forms:

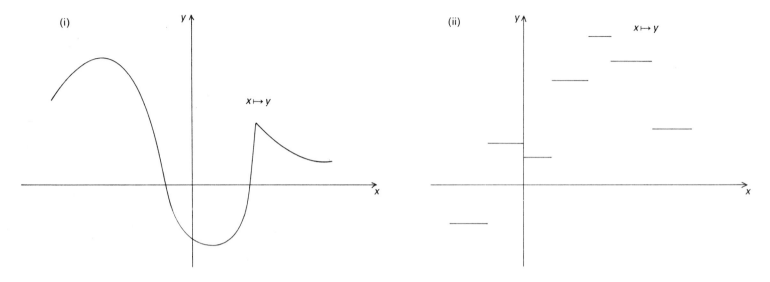

Figure 2.9   (i) A continuous graph; (ii) the graph of a step-function.

(i) Real situations are dealt with in chapters entitled *statistics*.

(ii) The work which leads towards functions and the idea of dependence is conducted in an abstract way, not relating the ideas to graphs which may occur outside mathematics.

If these two lines of thought could be fused so that Cartesian graphs, their equations and the idea of functional dependence could grow from children's primary-school experience of collecting, recording and interpreting information in a systematic way, so as to incorporate the graphs of measured data which pupils draw in other subjects, this would be a great improvement.

3 The Idea of a Function

3.1. Dependence

The idea of a *function* is one of the basic ideas of mathematics and is particularly important in the uses of mathematics in the real world. It is derived in the first place from the fact that a quantity may *depend on* one or more other quantities. As such, it is a very familiar aspect of everyday life, which does not have to be artificially introduced into children's thinking. They know that the price they pay for sweets depends on how many packets they buy, that the BBC 1 television programme which is showing depends on the time of day, that whether it is school or holiday time depends on the time of year, and so on. In the secondary school, teachers introduce their pupils to many functions: the science teacher shows them that the length of a spring depends on the mass hung from it, and that the pressure exerted by a given volume of gas depends on its temperature; the geography teacher discusses the fact that the local time depends on the time zone in which a place is situated; the physical education teacher demonstrates how the distance travelled by a cricket ball depends on a number of aspects of the thrower's action, such as the angle at which the ball is thrown. In mathematics we expect our pupils to notice that the area of a rectangle depends on its length and its breadth, that the distance a ladder reaches up a wall depends on its angle to the floor, that the area of a circle depends on its radius; and we find many other examples of dependence throughout mathematics.

The concept of *function* grew in order to express mathematically this notion of *dependence*. For users of mathematics, as well as for mathematicians, it is one of the key ideas, for so much of both mathematics and science is concerned with studying how one thing depends on another. Hence all pupils in the 11–16 age group should meet activities which will enable them to develop the idea of functional dependence. From these examples will emerge the generality and power of functional dependence, and of the uses which are made of functions in mathematics and other subjects. Like the man who discovered that he had spoken prose all his life, the pupil needs to discover that he is surrounded by functions, whose behaviour he can begin to analyse mathematically.

For some pupils, their ideas of functional dependence will remain simple, pictorial, and mostly qualitative:

> The bigger the block of chocolate, the more it costs.
> The time it gets dark in the evening depends on the time of the year.

The majority of pupils will be able to understand that different types of functional dependence are expressed by graphs of different shapes, and to realize the significance of a linear function:

> Doubling the weight of chocolate doubles the price.

They will by age sixteen be able to attach a good deal of significance to the steepness of straight-line and other graphs. For some students, the building-up of a vocabulary of different types of functional dependence will be a necessary preparation for future work. They will need to recognize quadratic as well as linear functions, and to realize the significance of inverse as well as direct proportion.

3.2. Historical Development of the Idea of a Function

Like many other important ideas, the idea of a function has gradually been refined and clarified over the years, and has only fairly recently been seen in its full generality. It is important that teachers should be aware of this change, for even some recent texts which they may use or consult may be based on outmoded definitions of a function. Moreover, in the last few years some school texts have adopted a point of view about functions which does not seem to help pupils to realize their importance. We therefore now discuss the historical development of the function idea, and how this is reflected in school texts.

The following early definitions show how mathematicians groped to make their ideas of a function more precise.

> A quantity composed in any manner of a variable and any constants. (Jean Bernoulli, 1718)
> Any analytic expression whatsoever made up from that variable quantity and from numbers or constant quantities. (Euler, 1748)
> Quantities dependent on others, such that as the second change, so do the first, are said to be functions. (Euler)
> If a variable y is related to a variable x, so that whenever a numerical value is assigned to x there is a rule according to which a *unique* value of y is determined, then y is said to be a function of the independent variable x. (Dirichlet, 1837)

These early definitions reached out to express in words the idea of the dependence of one quantity on another, together with the idea that the second quantity is *uniquely* determined from the first by some *rule*.

At first, this rule had to be expressed in a single formula, but by the time of Dirichlet the single algebraic formula had been found to be too restrictive. For example, if x is a counting number greater than 1, the rule

$$y \text{ is the highest prime factor of } x$$

gives rise to a perfectly good function, according to Dirichlet's definition, although the rule is expressed in words rather than symbols.

Unfortunately, as time went on, Dirichlet's definition, which is so suitable as a basis for the classroom introduction of functions, was modified in the search for further generality. Nearly a century later we read in Hardy's great textbook *Pure Mathematics* (1908):

> All that is essential (to a function) is that there should be some relation between x and y such that to some values of x at any rate correspond values of y.

Hardy had abandoned the idea that a unique y should depend on each x. This admitted "many-valued functions" to mathematics, so that to Hardy $y^2 = 1 - x^2$ was a function, but had the property that if $x = 0$, then $y = +1$ or -1. This generalization has been rejected by later writers, who have returned to Dirichlet's statement that a function is obtained by giving a *rule* whereby *exactly one* y is obtained from *each* admissible x.

Modern writers have also realized the importance of the *set* from which the admissible values of x are drawn and the *set* from which the values of y are drawn, so that in elementary modern treatments the concept of a function is developed so as to have three constituent parts:

(i) a starting set, called the *domain* of the function, whose members are the admissible values of x;

(ii) a target set, called the *codomain* of the function, a single member of which is attached to each x;

(iii) a set of arrows or a *rule*, to show which member of the codomain depends on each member of the domain.

This idea of a function is shown diagrammatically in figure 3.1, and is very simple and suitable for development with pupils

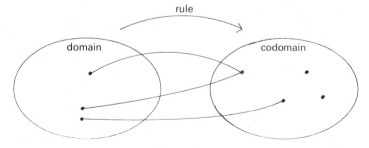

Figure 3.1

between 11 and 16. The rule expresses the functional dependence. For example, the area of a circle of radius r is πr^2; the rule is

$$r \text{ maps to } \pi r^2.$$

This rule is easily given by a formula, but many rules are not. For the height of a growing plant (section 2.1), the rule is that the number of weeks since planting maps to the height of the plant.

3.3. Elementary Notation and Wording

It is convenient to have a standard vocabulary for describing functions, which can gradually be built up with pupils. Most people talk about the arrow in figure 3.2 as "3 maps to 9" or "3 goes

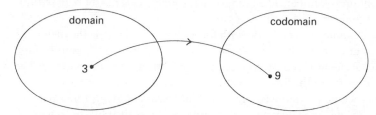

Figure 3.2

to 9". If the rule is that each member of the domain maps to its square, we can say more generally that, for a given member x of the domain,

$$x \text{ maps to } x^2.$$

This is often written

$$x \to x^2$$

or

$$x \mapsto x^2.$$

In this book the second of these notations is used.

A more general function is shown in figure 3.3. Here we write $x \mapsto f(x)$. The use of $f(x)$ to denote the member of the codomain to which x maps is becoming more general in texts intended for pupils up to the age of 16, as is the use of a single letter such as f to represent a function.

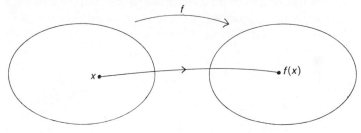

Figure 3.3

3.4. Use of the Word *function* in "Traditional" Texts

Many books still in use in schools show considerable traces of older views of function; so does the vocabulary of many teachers. Pupils may be seriously confused when the teacher's colloquial expressions are not in accordance with the "modern" definitions which he uses.

Durell is a typical author of the "traditional" school, and his usage is well represented by the following quotation from *A New Algebra for Schools* (p. 157), written in 1930:

> Since this graph represents the relation between a number x and its square x^2, it is called the **graph of the function** x^2.
>
> Any expression, containing x, whose value can be found when the value of x is given, is called a **function** of x. Thus $7x$, $\frac{3}{4}x - 5$, $\frac{2x-1}{x+3}$, $x^3 - 5x$, etc., are all functions of x. The letter y is generally used to represent the function of x.

For Durell, as for Hardy and all his predecessors, *the formula was the function*. They talked about "the function $7x$". So do many teachers at the present time. However, most modern authors regard $7x$ as the member of the codomain of the function which corresponds to the member x of the domain (figure 3.4). Thus, in modern usage, the function which Durell spoke about as "the function $7x$" consists of:

    (i) a *domain*, which is usually assumed to be the set of real numbers, if there is no statement to the contrary;

    (ii) a *codomain*, which again is usually assumed to be the set of real numbers;

    (iii) the *rule*: $x \mapsto 7x$.

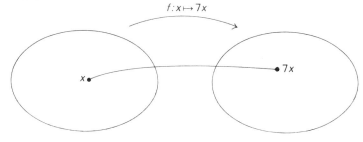

Figure 3.4

Many teachers have been brought up to speak of "the function $7x$" and it requires considerable concentration in the classroom to replace this in everyday speech by

the function: x maps to $7x$.

The view that the formula is the function persisted in school textbooks for many years, so that in 1959 Channon and McLeish Smith wrote, in *General Mathematics Book 4*, p. 152:

> Any algebraic expression which involves the variable x (and no other variable) is called a **function of x**, and its value depends on the value of x. The symbol used is $f(x)$, which is read as "function of x"; $f(2)$ means "the same expression with 2 written instead of x", $f(-1)$ means "the same expression with -1 written instead of x", and so on.

Thus, traditional authors, by emphasizing the formula for a function, emphasized the idea of *functional dependence*. Unfortunately, the words "the function $7x$" lose the idea of *mapping*. It is x which maps to $7x$, and this vitally important link between x and its image $7x$ needs emphasis for young pupils. We need to say

the function: x maps to $7x$

and to write

$$x \mapsto 7x.$$

Moreover, the suppression in traditional texts of the domain or the codomain of the function sometimes leads to difficulties over the use of functions as models of real situations.

For example, a function with rule $x \mapsto x^2$ models the areas of squares which can be built with the rods of structural apparatus. But this model only applies to structural apparatus when x is a natural number. The domain of the function is the set **N** of natural numbers.

Similarly, a function with formula $s = 5t^2$ models the distance s metres fallen in time t seconds by a stone dropped from the hand, but the model only applies to the situation when t is positive. The domain of the function is the set of positive real numbers.

Thus, the modern view of a function as having three parts, a *domain*, a *codomain* and a *rule*, is most helpful to pupils in understanding the power of the function concept, and how functions are used in modelling real situations. This development of the meaning of the word *function* in school mathematics started with the introduction of modern mathematics texts in the early 1960s.

However, the treatment of function in most modern texts has been greatly influenced by another mathematical point of view which seems to be unhelpful for young pupils, and so to be regrettable. This is described in chapter 5.

4 Functions in the Early Secondary Years

4.1. The Introduction of Functions

The idea of *functional dependence* will have been taught by using examples in which the members of one set depend on the members of another set (sections 1.3 and 3.1).

More examples can be found within the mathematics in the classroom. Some are:

  (i) The image of a point mapped by a reflection depends on which point is mapped.
 (ii) When a square is enlarged, the perimeter of the enlargement depends on the scale-factor.
(iii) The volume of a cube depends on the length of the edge.
 (iv) Each arithmetic operation produces examples of functional dependence. In the "seven times table", the answer depends on the starting number—the answer is always 7 times the starting number.

Straight-line models are appropriate in (ii) and (iv).

In science, and in other subjects, further examples of functional dependence are studied. For instance, in *Nuffield Physics Book 1*, different masses are hung from the ends of springs and elastic bands, and measurements are made (including testing to destruction). The model of a straight-line graph is not a good fit near the elastic limit.

In all these examples, ideas about functions can be brought out in discussion or exercises.

For example, figure 4.1 shows how the airmail postage for a letter to America depends on its mass in grams in 1976.

The following questions apply to this graph:

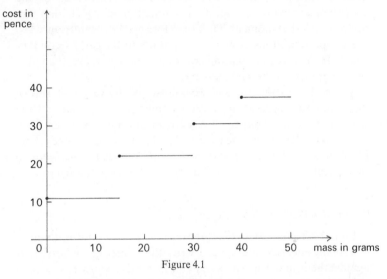

Figure 4.1

On what does the postage payable on a letter depend: its length and width, its mass, whether it is sealed?

What is the postage on a 35-gram letter?
What point does 20 map to?
What can we say about a letter which costs 30p?
What numbers can be mapped by the function?
What is the domain of the function?

4.2. Graphical Representation of Functions

Traditionally, the graphical representation of functions used in schools has been a Cartesian graph. Today several other methods of showing functions visually are available. Each of these pictures brings out particular features of the concept of function, and has its own strengths and weaknesses. Pupils should be able to choose from a variety of different representations, according to the particular function or aspect of a function in which they are interested at that moment. They therefore need to be introduced to these representations at appropriate times in the early secondary years. It is also illuminating for pupils to use more than one representation of the same function.

Some of the strengths and weaknesses of the various forms of diagrammatic representation are summarized below, so that the teacher can help pupils to choose the most appropriate one for a particular situation. The teacher will realize that some of the points listed do not apply to 11 and 12-year-old pupils, but he needs to help pupils to build up a vocabulary which they will use later.

(i) *The basic arrow diagram*

Figure 4.2 emphasizes the three parts of a function: the domain, codomain and rule. Pupils can write the names of the sets used against them, and can express the rule in words on an arrow. This is the most general way of representing a function pictorially, for it

accommodates domains and codomains which have no particular structure, and so which need not be sets of numbers. Many pupils will have used it in the primary school.

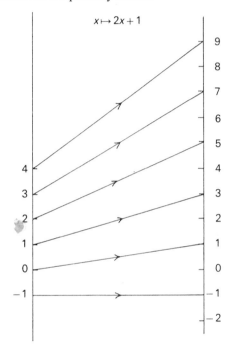

Figure 4.3

The main strengths of the basic arrow diagram are:
  (i) It is very simple indeed, so that it can be used with confidence by the least-able pupils.
 (ii) The domain and codomain need not be sets of numbers; this diagram can illustrate some examples for which other graphs fail, ranging from the names of pupils' pets to linear maps of vector spaces.

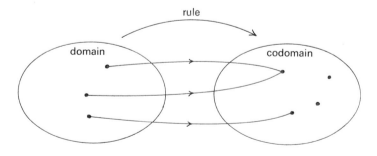

Figure 4.2

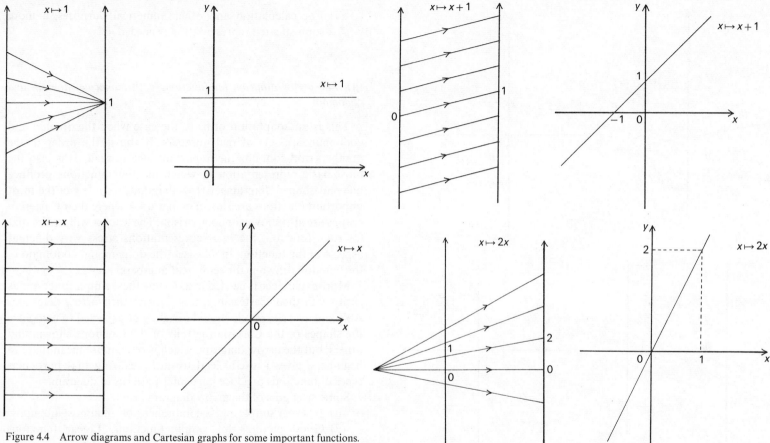

Figure 4.4   Arrow diagrams and Cartesian graphs for some important functions.

(iii) It brings out properties of the function, such as one-one, onto and the existence of an inverse function.

(iv) It shows composite functions very easily.

(v) It gives a diagrammatic representation of the most general function without any special features.

Its main weaknesses are:

(i) If the domain has a large number of members, the diagram is messy.

(ii) If the domain has an infinity of members, the diagram can only be symbolic of the function.

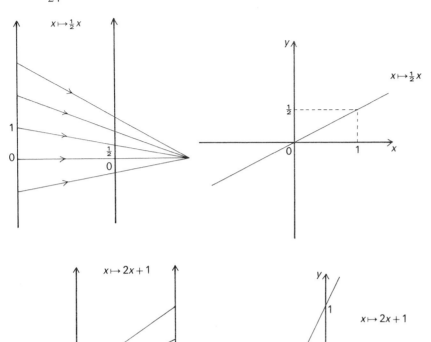

(v) For calculation and other numerical purposes, a more sophisticated representation is needed.

(ii) The arrow diagram for functions with numerical domain and codomain

This is an adaptation of (i) to the case when the domain and codomain are sets of real numbers. It shows the order of the numbers and contains the important idea of scale. It is also the most basic representation in which different functions produce different-shaped diagrams. Arrow diagrams for a few of the most important functions are shown in figure 4.4, where their Cartesian graphs are also shown for comparison. The teacher will realize that for each function, the two representations stress very different aspects of the function. In all cases, the domain and codomain of the function drawn is the set of real numbers.

More experience is needed to associate these simple functions as easily with their Cartesian graphs as with their arrow diagrams. Able and average pupils should certainly be expected to recognize the shapes of the Cartesian graphs of the functions shown, and others, but the arrow diagram, which is often more meaningful to beginners, gives a useful lead towards realizing that particular types of functions produce particular patterns of diagram.

Some strengths of the arrow diagram are:
  (i) It is very simple and is comprehensible to almost all pupils.
  (ii) Good pictures for simple functions. Linear functions connect easily with transformation geometry.
  (iii) The order of the numbers is emphasized. Functions which preserve order are distinguished from those which do not.
  (iv) The diagram for a composite function is easily constructed.
  (v) The diagram for the inverse function (if any) is easily constructed.
  (vi) It brings out whether the function is one-one or many-

  (iii) If the domain and codomain are subsets of the real numbers, the diagram does not show the order of the numbers.
  (iv) It does not attach a shape of picture to any particular function.

one.

(vii) The derivative of the function is meaningful as the local scale-factor (but see chapter 14).

Its weaknesses can be summarized as:

(i) It can only be symbolic of the function unless the domain has a finite number of members.

(ii) Unless the function is of the form $x \mapsto mx + c$, the diagram may become messy.

(iii) There is no representation of the integral of the function.

(iii) *The Cartesian graph*

The Cartesian graph is the most familiar of all the illustrations of a function. Hence, it is very difficult for a teacher to look at it with

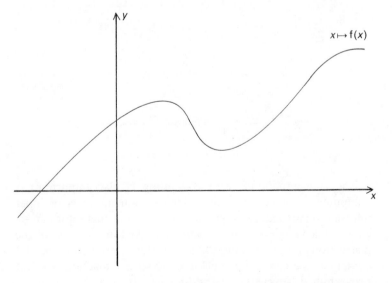

Figure 4.5

fresh eyes, and to realize how much building-up of concepts he brings to his own interpretation of a Cartesian graph. The reader should notice how automatically he himself draws a smooth curve through a few plotted points, the meaning he attaches to positive and negative gradients as indicating increasing and decreasing functions, the particular significance he gives to points of zero gradient, the range of knowledge he brings to the interpretation of straight-line graphs. At the beginning of their secondary-school education, pupils have none of these ideas available to them, and one of the most important tasks is the development of their grasp of the significance of different features of a Cartesian graph.

Some of the strengths of Cartesian graphs are:

(i) Familiarity. Cartesian graphs are a part of our culture, and pupils must learn to use and interpret them.

(ii) The order of the real numbers is clearly shown in both domain and codomain.

(iii) A knowledge of the shapes of Cartesian graphs of the commoner functions is an aspect of mathematical literacy.

(iv) The Cartesian graph is the only representation in which the concept of a continuous function is visually meaningful.

(v) Good for sum and difference functions, which are easily constructed.

(vi) The derivative is meaningful as the gradient of the graph.

(vii) The integral is meaningful as the area under the graph.

Its main weaknesses are:

(i) It only shows the mapping arrows implicitly, so it needs careful teaching in the early stages.

(ii) It can only be used when both the domain and codomain are sets of real numbers.

(iii) Pupils may think that the complete set of real numbers is the domain of every function.

(iv) It does not emphasize whether the function is one-one or many-one.

(v) The graph of the inverse function (if any) is not immediately obvious, although it can easily be found.

(vi) It is not good for composite functions, for which new graphs always have to be drawn.

(iv) *The "function machine"*

Figure 4.6

Many mathematical concepts are important because they have a number of different aspects which make them appropriate for use in different contexts. The idea of a function is one of these. Functions with particular formulae are used in modelling because rules found in real-life situations are usually approximately regular. The rule does the same to each element of the domain. For example, the function $x \mapsto 7x$ multiplies every number by 7. We can input any real number x, and the function outputs $7x$. The "function machine" diagram is important because it enables this *processing* aspect of a function to be made vivid to pupils. The pupil can imagine himself feeding the input of 5 into the "black box", which outputs 35. Any appropriate input of a member of the domain is *transformed* or *processed* by the function.

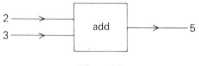

Figure 4.7

We often speak about the *processes of arithmetic*. Addition is a function which needs two inputs. If we feed in 2 and 3, the addition function produces 5. The function machine illustration is the only elementary diagram for this situation. It can also be used to focus

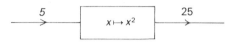

Figure 4.8

attention on the algebraic formulation of a functional rule (figure 4.8), and it shows composite and inverse functions very easily (figure 4.9).

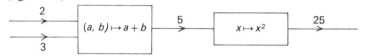

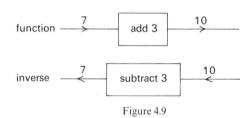

Figure 4.9

The conceptual link with computing is also important. A computer is a black box into which certain numbers or other information are fed. The computer prints out further information, which is a function of the input. The program consists of the instructions for the required function. Pupils need to think of a computer as a processing machine, and so as a machine which is programmed to generate the result of applying a function to an input.

4.3. The Labelling of Cartesian Graphs

In this book we have suggested that graphs be approached by keeping records of information obtained from real situations. A function may then be constructed to model the situation, and a Cartesian graph of the function may be drawn and studied. For instance, if a stone falls from the top of a cliff, the number of metres fallen in t seconds is fairly well modelled by the function with formula $t \mapsto 5t^2$, whose graph is shown in figure 4.10; a problem then arises about the labelling of the vertical axis.

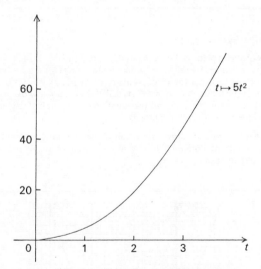

Figure 4.10   A function which models the vertical fall of a stone.

Some texts follow one of the policies illustrated in a general situation in figure 4.11, but these lead to difficulties if two functions are to be drawn on the same axes, and the second is particularly inappropriate in the case of a function such as $x \mapsto 1$.

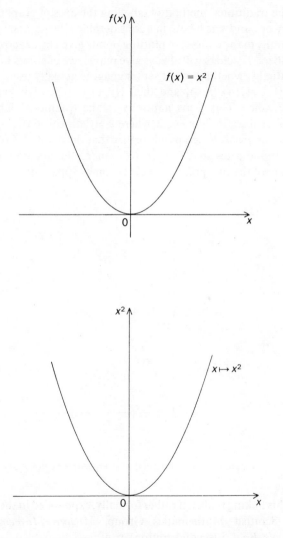

Figure 4.11   Labelling of the vertical axis: two recent usages.

The traditional method of labelling the axes of graphs, using x and y or t and s as labels, has considerable advantages, and arises naturally in the context of plotting points given by ordered pairs of numbers. Teachers will always give pupils sets of points to plot and eventually, whether or not set language is actually used, sets such as $\{(1, 2), (2, 4), (3, 6)\}$ and then $\{(x, y):y = 2x\}$, will make their appearance. This leads naturally to the traditional labelling of graphs shown in figure 4.12, where $y = 2x$ is called the *equation of the set* or *graph*. When pupils realize that the point $(3, 6)$ of the line $y = 2x$ indicates that 3 maps to 6 under the function $x \mapsto 2x$, a linking of the two points of view becomes apparent.

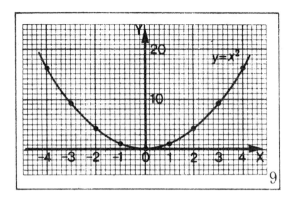

Note on the equation of a graph

The coordinate plane is the set of points defined by $\{(x, y):x \in R, y \in R\}$. Since a function is defined by the set of ordered pairs $\{(x, f(x)):x \in D\}$, where D is a subset of R, we consider the set of points given by $\{(x, y):y = f(x), x \in D\}$ to be the graph of the function f. $\quad y = f(x)$ is called the *equation of the graph* of f.

In the above example, $y = x^2$ is the equation of the graph of the function f for which $f(x) = x^2$, as shown in figure 9.

Example 1. Figure 10 shows the graph of the quadratic function f given by $f(x) = x^2 - 4x$, with domain $\{x: -2 \leqslant x \leqslant 6, x \in R\}$, i.e. the set of real numbers from -2 to 6 inclusive.

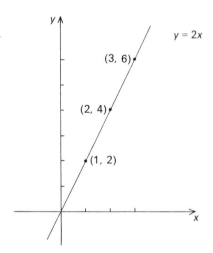

Figure 4.12   Labelling of the vertical axis: traditional usage.

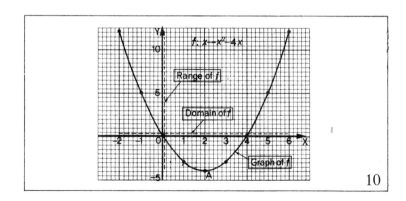

This linking is ably, if rather formally, expounded in the books of the Scottish Mathematics Group, *Modern Mathematics for Schools*, Book 5 (second edition), p. 58:

Thus both methods of labelling shown in figure 4.13 are acceptable practice and are convenient in different circumstances. In (i), the graph is labelled to show the *function* $x \mapsto x^2$, and in (ii) the *equation* $y = x^2$ of the graph of the function is emphasized.

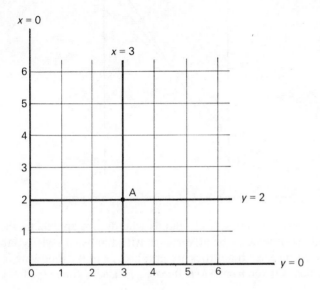

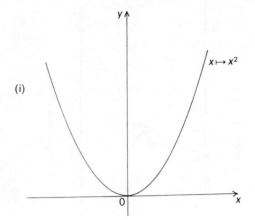

(i)

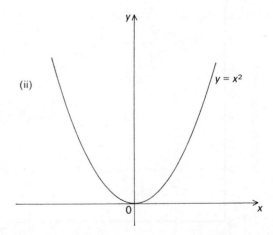

(ii)

Figure 4.13 Labelling of graphs: two acceptable practices.

In this book both notations will be used; whichever one is more convenient will be chosen for each particular example.

The writers of the *SMP* texts use a different style of labelling on the axes, as the illustration above shows (*Book A*, p. 21). Unfortunately, this style leads to considerable confusion in pupils' minds for, although the equation of the horizontal axis certainly is $y = 0$, the points $0, 1, 2, \ldots$ marked on it are values of x. Moreover,

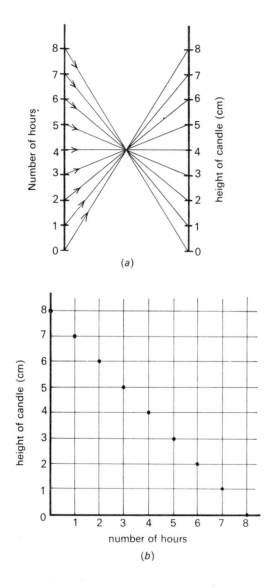

(a)

(b)

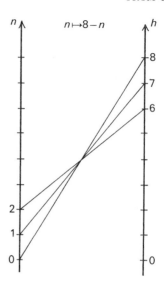

Figure 4.14   Labelling of an arrow graph.

the practice may seem to pupils who do not appreciate the finer points of logic to be at variance with the usual style of labelling when physical quantities are graphed, as in the following extract, which is taken from *SMP Book C, Teachers' Guide* (p. T97).

> If we let x stand for the number of hours and y for the height of the candle in cm, then the relation between x and y is
>
> $$x + y = 8 \quad \text{or} \quad x = 8 - y \quad \text{or} \quad y = 8 - x$$

If the height of the candle after n hours is h cm, the axes of the Cartesian graph could certainly be labelled $h = 0$ and $n = 0$, but no such labelling is possible for the arrow graph, although the labelling shown in figure 4.14 would still be possible.

An additional point which arises from the extract is the conflict of conventions between teachers of science and mathematics over the labelling of graphs. This controversy will no doubt continue to be bitterly fought out between science teachers, who teach that *h* stands for a height, and that the associated number is *h*/cm, and mathematics teachers, who usually insist that a letter stands for a number, and so write that the height of the candle is *h* cm. However, from either point of view, there seems little merit in

$$\text{height of candle (cm)},$$

when elsewhere in mathematics this use of a bracket denotes multiplication. Our more logical science colleagues write either

$$\text{height of candle in cm}$$

or

$$\text{height of candle/cm.}$$

5 Further Developments of the Function Idea

5.1. Introduction

We have seen that in "traditional" texts, a formula was regarded as a function. More "modern" texts, published since about 1960, regard a function as having three parts:

domain, *codomain* and *rule*.

In previous chapters, we have emphasized the importance of the idea of *functional dependence*. However, a number of modern texts treat functions very differently, regarding them as particular examples of *relations*.

This approach is unhelpful to pupils' understanding of functions, and should not be used for the reasons given in the next section.

5.2. Doing without the "Rule"

The treatment of functions as special cases of relations has its roots, as have all the previous developments of the idea of a function, in the advanced work of mathematicians. One of the three essential components of a function is the *rule*, which describes how each member of the domain maps to a member of the codomain.

In recent years some mathematicians, concerned with the logical and conceptual foundations of their subject, have taken the view that the use of the word *rule* begs questions. They have avoided the use of the idea of a rule and realized that all that is needed is a list of pairings, saying which member of the codomain is to be attached to each member of the domain. In figure 5.1, the list of pairings

$$a_1 \mapsto b_1, \quad a_2 \mapsto b_2, \quad a_3 \mapsto b_2$$

or

$$(a_1, b_1), \quad (a_2, b_2), \quad (a_3, b_2)$$

is quite sufficient to specify the function shown, without a verbal description of the rule. Indeed, no convenient verbal description of this rule exists. Hence, all that is needed to describe the function is a

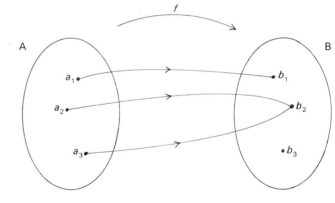

Figure 5.1

list of ordered pairs. When mathematicians define a function, they can do without the word "rule" and merely list the linked elements in ordered pairs.

This idea has given rise, in advanced work, to a treatment of the idea of a function which is more general and so might be considered to be more logically satisfactory. The order of presentation of ideas in this development (which avoids the idea of "rule") is as follows.

(i) The idea of a *set* is first studied.

(ii) The idea that two elements *a* and *b* can be put together to form an *ordered pair* (a, b) is introduced.

(iii) This enables the *Cartesian product* A × B of two sets A and B to be defined as the set of all ordered pairs (a, b) such that $a \in A, b \in B$.

(iv) A *relation* from A to B is defined to be a subset of A × B; that is, a relation is any set of ordered pairs (a, b) whose members are drawn from A and B respectively; all mention of the word "rule" is avoided by simply giving a list of pairs which would have been linked together by the rule.

(v) A *function f* with domain A and codomain B is now a relation from A to B with the additional property that *each* $a \in A$ is the first member of *exactly one* ordered pair belonging to the function.

Thus a function is a set of ordered pairs (a, b) such that

(a) the first member *a* of each pair belongs to A,

(b) the second member *b* of each pair belongs to B,

(c) *each* member of A belongs to *exactly one* ordered pair of the function and so is uniquely attached to a single member of B.

In other words a function can be considered as a particular type of relation.

This definition of a function is logically satisfactory in an axiomatic development of mathematics in which the aim is to present each concept in terms of those ideas which have been previously defined.

Unfortunately, the idea of functional *dependence* has been totally eliminated from this formal definition of a function. In the process of generalization, the *rule* which was the essential idea of the function has vanished.

Inquiries among mathematicians who use functions as basic tools of their thinking show that working mathematicians usually think of functions as *rules* for mapping, rather than as sets of ordered pairs. *It is only when they need the logic of an axiomatic development that working mathematicians discard the idea of a rule in favour of a subset of A × B.*

Children of 12 and 13 years of age are not yet concerned with the logic of axiomatic development. They are still learning the tools of the mathematician's trade. When teaching beginners about functions, it is very unwise to suppress the idea that *functional dependence* is expressed by a *rule* for mapping. Functions are so important in their own right that they should not be taught as particular (and perhaps unimportant) types of relations. Functions are used as mathematical models in situations where *dependence* needs to be expressed. In many "modern" texts this idea is not clearly brought out.

The introduction of "modern" work, as at present seen, has not improved pupils' understanding of the key concept of a function. In traditional texts, functional ideas were introduced late, and the point of view used was not in accordance with the present mainstream of mathematical thinking. By contrast, the "modern" orthodoxy is to introduce functions early, but to minimize their importance. This seems very odd.

5.3. Review of Texts

The changes described above have only become part of the common currency of mathematics within the last twenty years, so that different texts in use in schools today show different stages of historical growth. Moreover, different authors have adopted different definitions for the same words, leading to a most unfortunate state of confusion.

The date of publication is no guide to the view of functions taken by an author. The latest editions of Durell still firmly hold that the formula is the function (C. V. Durell, *Certificate Mathematics*, Volume 2 (p. 150), second edition, 1971).

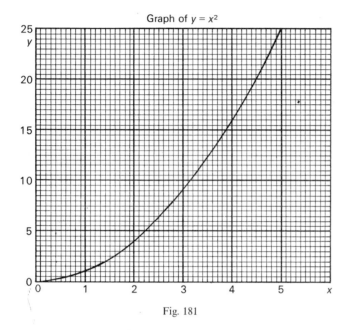

Fig. 181

The graph in figure 181 represents the relation between a number x and its square x^2: it is called the **graph of the function x^2**. Figure 181 also represents the graph of y, where $y = x^2$, for values of x from 0 to 5.

Channon, McLeish Smith and Head (*New General Mathematics 4* (1971) p. 102) use both the "particular relation" and the "function is the formula" views.

Functional notation

A many-to-one relation is called a **function**.

As a one-to-one relation, often called a **one-to-one correspondence**, is a special case of a many-to-one relation, it is also a function.

Any algebraic expression which involves the variable x (and no other variable) is a **function of x**, and its value depends on the value of x. The symbol used is $f(x)$, which is read as "function of x"; $f(2)$ means "the same expression with 2 written instead of x", $f(-1)$ means "the same expression with -1 written instead of x", and so on.

SMP Books 1 to 5 were among the first "modern" texts. For their authors, a function was a particular relation (*SMP Book 2* (1966) p. 158).

> A *relation* is a connection between members of two sets or members of the same set. Figure 8 represents the relation "has the prime factor" between the sets
>
> $$\{4, 6, 7, 15, 16, 20\} \quad \text{and} \quad \{2, 3, 5, 7\}.$$
>
> We can call this relation a *mapping*, saying that each number is mapped onto its prime factors. The set on the left in figure 8 is called the *domain*.
> A mapping is a *function* if each member of the *domain* has only one image, for example, the mapping which maps each number onto its smallest prime factor is a function.
> Figure 9 shows this mapping for the two sets above. Only one arrow starts from each member of the domain. The image set $\{2, 3, 7\}$ is called the *range*.
> The mapping represented in Figure 8 is not a function. The range in this case is $\{2, 3, 5, 7\}$.

Another word appeared in these texts: *SMP*, at that time, used *mapping* as another word for relation. They said that a mapping was a function if *each* member of the domain had a *unique* image.

Writing at about the same time, Mansfield and Bruckheimer in *Book 4* of *Mathematics: A New Approach* (1965), which is also in the "particular relation" school, avoided both words *relation* and *function*, using the word *mapping* for what is usually called a relation, and described functions as *one-one or many-one mappings* (*Mathematics: A New Approach, Pupil's Book 4* (1965), pp. 10–11).

> Any system by which every member of one set called the *domain set* (in the above example, the set of numbers of therms) has associated with it a member of another set called the *range set* (in the above example, the set of gas bills) is called a mapping.
> The only necessity in a mapping is that every member of the first set should have an image and that the mapping should provide a means of finding that image. We can, indeed, have mappings where a member of the domain has several different images. These mappings are called *one-many*.

In the *Teacher's Book 4*, they explained their policy. They were aware of the changing use of the word *function*, and attempted to

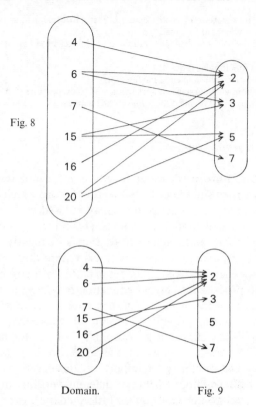

Fig. 8

Domain.   Fig. 9

were appearing, the following discussion of relations, mappings and functions appeared in *SMP Book D, Teachers' Guide* (1970), p. T231:

> The following definitions of the different types of mappings are included for the benefit of the teacher.
> A relation is many to one if the image of each element of the domain is a single element of the range. A relation is one to many if the inverse image of each element of its range is a single element of the domain. A relation is one to one if it is both many to one and one to many. A relation is many to many if it is neither one to many nor many to one.
> (iv) The relation 'is the brother of' defined on the set of brothers and sisters {Jane, Janet, June, Jack} is an example of a one to many correspondence.
> Many to one and one to one relations are mappings.
> It might be worth noting here that, in this course, unlike the SMP O-level course, we have chosen to use the more commonly recognized definition of a mapping: that is, a relation in which each member of the domain is related to one and only one member of the codomain. This statement corresponds to the definition of a function given in *Book 2*, p. 158, and the authors have decided that in *Books A–H*, in order to keep the mathematical language as simple as possible, the use of the word 'function' is therefore unnecessary.

Thus, in this series of texts, a mapping is a synonym for a function, rather than for a relation. This usage is in accordance with the usual meaning attached to the words *map* and *mapping* in advanced work, when a *mapping is always a function* (except in the texts of the Open University). However, functions have now been downgraded almost out of existence in the SMP lettered books.

The word *range* has also caused problems. Mansfield and Bruckheimer use *range* for the set which we have described as the codomain (*Mathematics: A New Approach, Pupil's Book 4*, p. 10).

> For example, consider the set of all the people in a town as domain. Map each person onto the number of hairs on his head. The range is the set of natural numbers and zero.

It is more usual to adopt the policy of *SMP Book D*, and to reserve the word *range* for the set of actual images, which is a subset of the codomain.

The definitions and notation used by the Scottish Mathematics Group are in accordance with those usual in advanced work. The

resolve the dilemma by avoiding the word (*Mathematics: A New Approach, Teacher's Book 4* (1965), p. 16).

> It is becoming common practice to use the word 'function' for one-one and many-one mappings only. Since this usage is not universal and some authors still use such phrases as 'many-valued functions' (which, in the new use of the word 'function', is a contradiction in terms), the word is not used in this book. It is not necessary, of course: the more general 'mapping' is entirely adequate.

Unfortunately, the word *mapping* has also been used with a variety of meanings, so that in 1970, when the *SMP* "letter" books first section of *Modern Mathematics for Schools, Book 5*, chapter 3 (second edition, 1973) is headed "Mappings, or functions". The authors are still members of the "particular relation" school, although they emphasize the importance of functions. This approach to functions also necessitates their very late introduction—in this case not until *Book 5* . The following extract is the key to what follows (*MMS Teacher's Book 5* (1973), pp. 50–51).

1 *Mappings, or functions*

In Book 3, we looked at some relations and mappings from one set to another set. In the present chapter, we develop these ideas further and study the important concept of *function*.

Example 1. Let $A = \{1, 4, 9\}$ and $B = \{1, 2, 3, 4\}$. Show in an arrow diagram the following relations from A to B:

(i) *is greater than*   (ii) *is the square of*

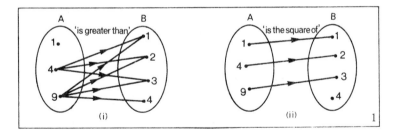

In (ii), the relation is a mapping since each element of A is related to exactly one element of B as is shown in figure 1(ii) where one arrow leaves each element of A.

Relations which are mappings are of prime importance in mathematics and are often referred to as *functional relations*, or simply *functions*. A function is therefore another name for a mapping. Both terms are useful; the idea of a mapping as a kind of operation helps to give a picture of a function.

A *function*, or *mapping*, from a set A to a set B is a relation in which each element of A is related to exactly one element of B. We write $A \to B$ (A maps to B).

Notation: If a function f maps an element x of set A to an element y of set B, we write $f : x \to y$, which may be read "f maps x to y".

y is called the *image* of x under f, and the set of images form the *range* of the function.

Thus for a function we require:

(i) a set A, called the *domain* of the function;

(ii) a relation which assigns each element of A to exactly one element of B. The set of images in B is called the *range* of the function.

5.4. Recommendations

The nomenclature used about functions in school texts has become very varied since about 1960, so that a word which is used with one meaning in one set of texts may be used with another (different) meaning in another set of texts. This causes considerable confusion for pupils and teachers alike. Pupils frequently change schools and texts, and good teachers consult more than one text, and often draw exercises from a number of places. Moreover, many students who proceed into higher education may have to modify their vocabulary at the beginning of their course. There seems no good reason for the present confusion of vocabulary to be perpetuated. When choosing a vocabulary for school use, the vividness with which it conveys the ideas to beginners, its memorability and its clarity are important considerations. There seems very little to choose between different versions on these grounds, so that this criterion gives little guidance, except that phrases such as

3 maps to 21

give a vivid dynamic picture of what is happening, and should be preserved.

In higher mathematics there is a considerable measure of agreement about the vocabulary of functions, and confusion would be diminished if this vocabulary were universally adopted. It is illustrated diagrammatically in figure 5.2.

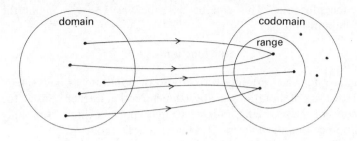

Figure 5.2   The vocabulary of functions: *every* member of the domain has *exactly* one arrow starting from it; the set of images is called the *range* of the function.

The variety of uses of the noun *mapping* and the verb *to map* in school mathematics presents particular difficulty as they have both been used in connection with both functions and relations.

In advanced work, the noun *mapping* (sometimes abbreviated to *map*) is only used to refer to functions (except in texts of the Open University) and its use in schools should also be confined to functions. Similarly the verb *to map* should be confined to functions or mappings, and used as a vivid way of talking about the mapping arrow in sentences such as "Each person *maps* to the number of hairs on his head".

The use of the verb *to map* in connection with relations should be avoided. The words *is related to* can always replace the words *maps to* in relations, and so reduce the danger of ambiguity. For example, consider the relation "is joined to" illustrated in figure 5.3. It is better to say "B is related to D" than "B maps to D".

Thus we concur with the following recommendations of the Teaching Committee of the Mathematical Association (*Mathematical Gazette* 418, December 1977):

> There are considerable difficulties in the definition of some of the common terms; our aim is to suggest a scheme which is usable in the sixth form, with obvious consequences at earlier stages.
>
> The idea of a relation is a very general one in mathematics. For school we make the following recommendations.

A *relation* associates some elements of a first set—the *domain*—with some elements of a second (or the same) set—the *codomain*.

A *function* associates with each element of the domain one and only one element of the codomain. The elements of the codomain which are "images" of elements of the domain form a subset of the codomain—the *range* of the function. Thus we may have a "many-valued relation" but not a "many-valued function".

We recommend that *mapping* be synonymous with function.

Another major problem of notation for functions has no clear solution. For us, a function has three parts: the domain, the codomain and the rule. We have abandoned Durell's view that the

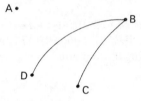

Figure 5.3

formula is the function. We should no longer speak of "the function $7x$". In advanced work, a new notation has grown up to describe such a function. Many mathematicians write

$$f : \mathbf{R} \to \mathbf{R} \quad \text{given by} \quad f(x) = 7x$$

to express the function with domain the set of real numbers $\mathbf{R}$, codomain $\mathbf{R}$ and rule $x \mapsto 7x$. This is unwieldy for everyday use by beginners, who are often not interested in the domain and codomain as much as they are in the rule. In this case it is better to use the abbreviated form of words

the function $x \mapsto 7x$ (the function x maps to $7x$)

or if the function needs a name:

the function $f : x \mapsto 7x$
(the function f under which x maps to $7x$).

This notation has already been adopted in the majority of modern school texts, and presents no difficulty to the learner.

However, the Mathematical Association recommendations continue:

> A function may be denoted by a single letter f. Generally by $f(x)$ we mean that element of the range which is the image of the element x of the domain under the function f, but it is sometimes convenient to use $f(x)$ in an "old-fashioned" way to describe the function itself (usually where a particular function is involved, e.g. "the function $x^2 - 3x + 2$").
>
> The arrow $\rightarrow$ is used to mean both "is mapped onto" and "tends to". Usually there is little chance of confusion, but if distinction is necessary the "barred arrow" $\mapsto$ may be used to indicate that an element of the domain is mapped to an element of the codomain.

The problem referred to in the second sentence is that a general function can be described by a single letter f, but there is no equally brief way of describing the function which maps each number to its cube plus one. This can be described as $x \mapsto x^3 + 1$, but the temptation to say

$$\text{the function } x^3 + 1$$

is strong, and certainly this "abuse of notation" is convenient. However, if notation is abused before the learner grasps the concept he is being taught, it may prevent him from fully appreciating the concept. It is better to talk about

$$\text{the function } x \text{ maps to } x^3 + 1$$

until the learner is thoroughly familiar with the constituent parts of a function: domain, codomain, and rule. Thus, the "abuse of notation" which talks about "the function $7x$" should be avoided before the age of 16.

6 Some Special Graphs

6.1. Straight-Line Graphs and Proportionality

Functions whose graphs are straight lines through the origin turn up so often as models of situations in the real world that a particular jargon has developed to describe them, and is used as everyday language by scientists and mathematicians. This jargon

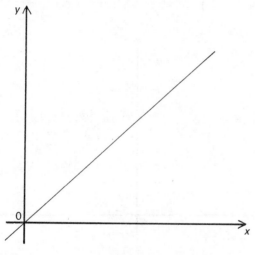

Figure 6.1

of *proportionality* needs to be known by pupils, who often do not realize that they are dealing with linear functions under a different guise.

A straight line through the origin is a graphical model which describes either exactly or approximately many everyday phenomena, and can be easily used to make predictions about them. For example, x might represent the number of kilometres travelled by a car on a motorway and y the number of litres of petrol used; or x might be the number of people in a household and £y the cost of their food per day.

In the first case the car may travel about 10 kilometres for each litre of petrol, and $y = \frac{1}{10}x$ is then the equation of the graph used as a model. However, in this situation x can only take positive values, and so we are concerned with the function $x \mapsto \frac{1}{10}x$ with domain the non-negative numbers.

In the second case, if it costs about 50p per day to feed a person, then $y = \frac{1}{2}x$. It is obvious that this statement is only approximately true, for not everyone eats the same amount of food, and it is also clear that x must be a positive integer or zero. However, $y = \frac{1}{2}x$, although only an approximation, acts as a mathematical model which says something useful about the cost of running a household.

These graphs and functions are often described in the language of proportionality

$$y \text{ is directly proportional to } x$$

or

$$y \text{ is proportional to } x.$$

The two examples above are often described as "the petrol used by a car on the motorway is proportional to the distance travelled" and "the cost of the food used in a household is proportional to the number of people in the household".

More precisely, the statement that "*y is directly proportional to x*" means that $y = kx$ for some fixed value of k. In the cases in which the statement "y is directly proportional to x" is used, the domain is the set of values of x which are appropriate to the situation being described. Moreover, k is positive in cases in which the language of proportion is used.

Pupils may mistakenly get the impression that all straight-line graphs are described by "y is proportional to x", and teachers may need to emphasize that it is only straight lines through the origin which correspond to direct proportion.

Unfortunately, direct proportion is often taught as a purely arithmetical idea, divorced from its graphical illustration.

6.2. Other Examples of Proportionality

The idea of proportionality is also used to help pupils to think of non-linear functions in a way which connects them with linear functions. Examples can be taken from graphs such as $y = k\sqrt{x}$ and $y = kx^2$. In the first case, we may say that "y is (directly) proportional to the square root of x" or "y varies as the square root of x", and in the second case "y is proportional to the square of x" or "y varies as the square of x".

Examples of the use of the language of proportionality are "the distance of the horizon at sea is proportional to the square root of the height of the observer above sea-level" and "the distance fallen by a stone is proportional to the square of the time for which it has fallen". Here too, the domains of the functions may need consideration, and pupils should consider whether a good model of the situation has been made.

Appropriate language to describe situations modelled by the graphs of $y = k/x$ and $y = k/x^2$ is "y is inversely proportional to x" or "y varies inversely as x" and "y is inversely proportional to x^2" or "y varies inversely as x^2" respectively. Examples of these situations are:

(i) for rectangles of given area, the length is inversely proportional to the width;

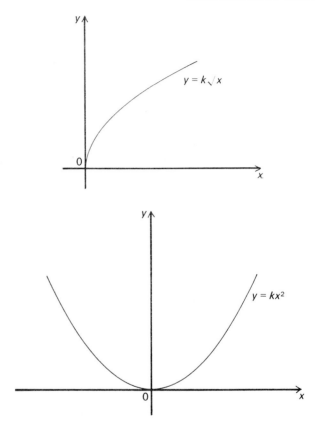

Figure 6.2

(ii) the force of attraction between the sun and a planet is inversely proportional to the square of the distance between them.

In the examples we have discussed, able students should eventually know what functions are used, should know the shapes

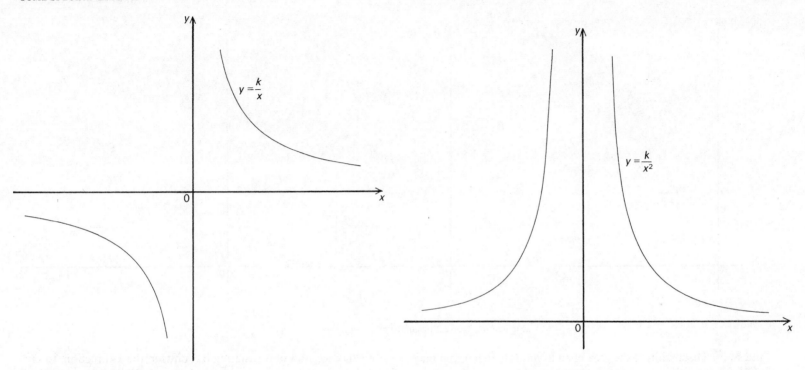

Figure 6.3

of the graphs of these functions, and should be aware that common sense should be used in the interpretation of the graph, both regarding the domain of the function and the suitability of the function as a model of the situation.

6.3. The Reciprocal Function

It is particularly important that the graph of $y = 1/x$, cor-responding to the function $x \mapsto 1/x$, should be known and recognized by pupils.

The calculator makes it easy to explore reciprocals numerically, so that $x \mapsto 1/x$ gives, for example,

$$2 \mapsto 0{\cdot}5$$
$$20 \mapsto 0{\cdot}05$$
$$200 \mapsto 0{\cdot}005$$
$$0{\cdot}2 \mapsto 5$$
$$0{\cdot}02 \mapsto 50$$

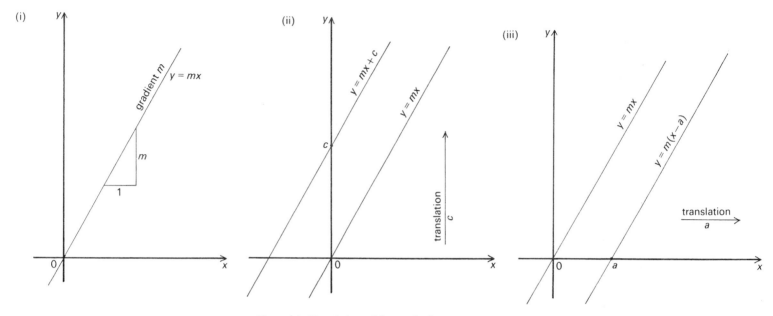

Figure 6.4   Translations of the graph of $y = mx$.

and so on. Discussion of the idea of an asymptote to a graph may well arise from this.

The calculator's error message also reinforces pupils' knowledge that 0 does not have a reciprocal, so that the domain of $x \mapsto 1/x$ cannot include 0.

6.4. Transformations of Some Common Graphs

Pupils who recognize the association between a straight-line graph through the origin, its gradient m, and its equation $y = mx$, should also see the effect on the equation of translating the graph c units in the y-direction to give the graph whose equation is $y = mx + c$, and of translating it a units in the x-direction, to give the graph whose equation is $y = m(x - a)$. While the first of these translations is usually taught, the second is equally important for a full understanding of the relation between the graph and its equation. Of course, most pupils below the age of sixteen will deal with these transformations largely in numerical terms.

Similarly, the general shape of the graph of the parabola of $y = x^2$ should be known, together with its translations $y = x^2 + c$ and $y = (x - a)^2$. These are shown in figure 6.5.

An enlargement in the y-direction is also an important transformation. If the scale-factor of the enlargement is k, then the parabola $y = x^2$ becomes $y = kx^2$, and the straight line $y = x$ becomes $y = kx$ (figure 6.6). Knowledge of these transformations

(i)

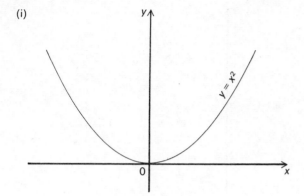

(ii)

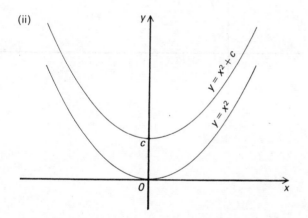

Figure 6.5   Translations of the graph of $y = x^2$.

(iii)

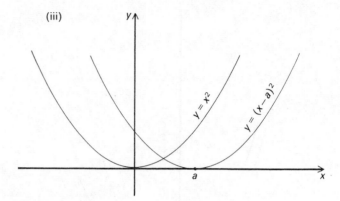

6.5. Graphs of the Sine and Cosine Functions

Some teachers prefer to introduce the sine and cosine functions using definitions for angles between 0° and 90° based on right-angled triangles. They then extend the definitions of sine and cosine to angles outside the range 0° to 90° in such a way that the new definition (i) agrees with the old one within 0° to 90°, and (ii) is seen by pupils to be a natural extension outside 0° to 90°. This is usually done by using a definition based on a circle of unit radius, centre (0, 0), in which a radius OP is drawn at an angle θ to the x-axis, and the sine and cosine functions are defined by the equations (figure 6.8)

$$\sin \theta = y$$
$$\cos \theta = x.$$

Other teachers prefer to begin by defining $\sin \theta$ and $\cos \theta$ for all angles, using the circle definition given above, and then to consider the trigonometry of the right-angled triangle as being concerned particularly with the values of θ between 0° and 90°.

Whichever order is chosen, a complete graph of the sine function cannot be drawn until it is defined for angles of all magnitudes.

should together enable the pupil to make a reasonable guess of $y = ax^2 + bx + c$ for the equation of a graph such as that of figure 6.7. Of course, these transformations can be used on all graphs, not merely straight lines and parabolas.

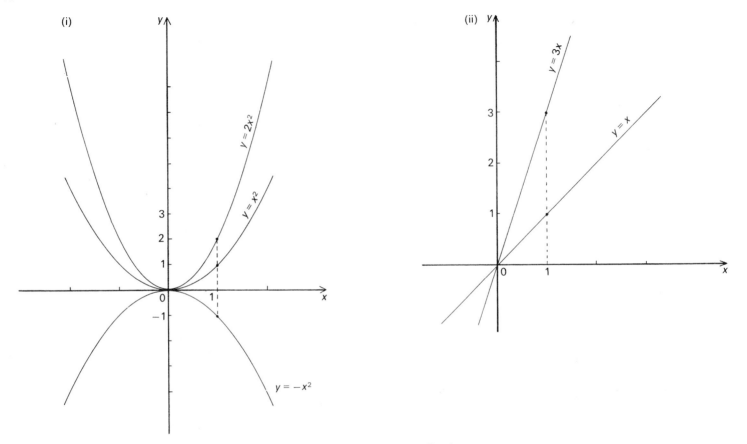

Figure 6.6   Enlargements in the y-direction.

Then its periodic nature will be appreciated. It is this property of periodicity which makes the sine function such a useful model for so many regularly recurring physical situations.

Pupils should know and be able quickly to sketch the sine and cosine graphs in figure 6.9 and should recognize the type of physical situation involving periodic motion for which they are good models.

Translations and enlargements along the x and y-axis are often

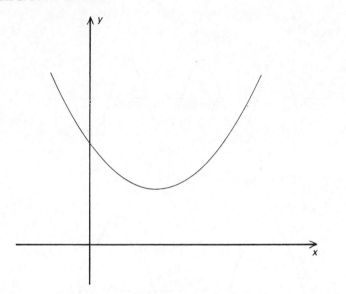

Figure 6.7

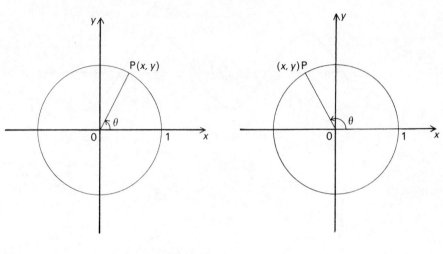

Figure 6.8

needed. Pupils will notice that the graph of $x \mapsto \sin x°$ is the graph of $x \mapsto \cos x°$ translated through $90°$ along the x-axis, so that

$$\sin x° = \cos (x - 90)°.$$

Enlargements are particularly important, for enlargement in the direction of the x-axis changes the wave-length, and enlargement in the direction of the y-axis changes the amplitude of the wave. For instance, the graph of figure 6.10(i) is obtained from $y = \sin x°$ by an enlargement scale-factor $\frac{1}{2}$ in the x-direction. Its equation is $y = \sin 2x°$.

Figure 6.10(ii) is obtained from $y = \sin x°$ by an enlargement scale-factor 2 in the y-direction. The equation is $y = 2\sin x°$, and the waves are twice as high, or have an amplitude twice that of $y = \sin x°$.

Figure 6.10(iii) shows the graph of $y = \sin (x - 30)°$ in which the whole wave has been shifted in the x-direction, or undergone a phase change, while figure 6.10(iv) shows $y = 2 + \sin x°$ in which the whole wave has been translated by two units in the y-direction.

Some examples of the uses of sine and cosine graphs in modelling are shown below.

The height of a bicycle pedal above the ground as the cycle is being pedalled can be modelled by a function with formula of the type

$$h = 25 + 15 \sin (360t)°$$

where t is the time in seconds from the time of starting, and h is the height in centimetres. The graph of this is shown in figure 6.11.

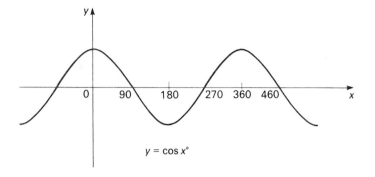

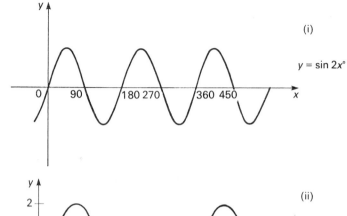

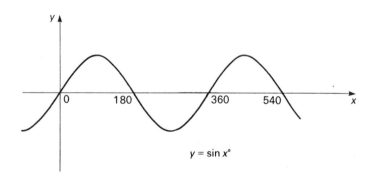

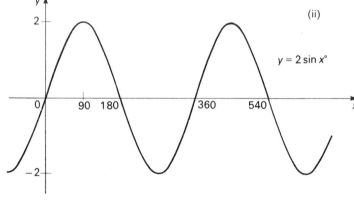

Figure 6.9   Graphs of $y = \cos x°$ and $y = \sin x°$.

Figure 6.10   Transformations of the graph of $y = \sin x°$. (i) $y = \sin 2x°$; (ii) $y = 2 \sin x°$; (iii) $y = \sin(x - 30)°$; (iv) $y = 2 + \sin x°$.

The distance of the bob of a pendulum from the vertical position after time t seconds may be given by a formula such as

$$x = 5 \cos (2\pi t)°$$

and the graph is that of figure 6.12.

Other examples are the variation in the length of daylight through the year, the bobbing up and down of a cork on a wave,

and the slower movement up and down of tides. All these are modelled by sine or cosine graphs which have been transformed from the basic graphs of figure 6.9.

6.6. The Exponential Function

The exponential function arises from the attempt by mathema-

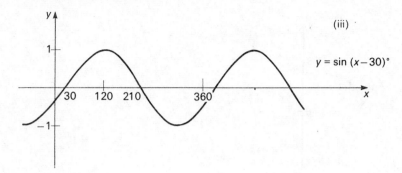

(iii)

$y = \sin(x-30)°$

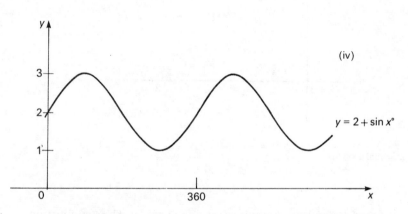

(iv)

$y = 2 + \sin x°$

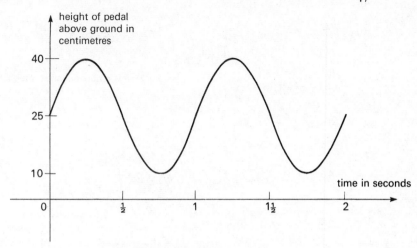

Figure 6.11   The height of a bicycle pedal.

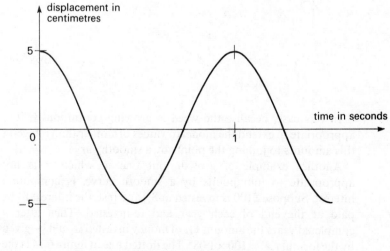

Figure 6.12   The displacement of a pendulum bob.

ticians to find a function which models a commonly-occurring type of growth.

Consider the mythical pond-weed which doubles its area every day. On the first day its area is 1 cm². What is its area after x days? A mathematical model gives its area y cm² after x complete days by the formula

$$y = 2^x$$

This is shown in figure 6.13(i).

(i)

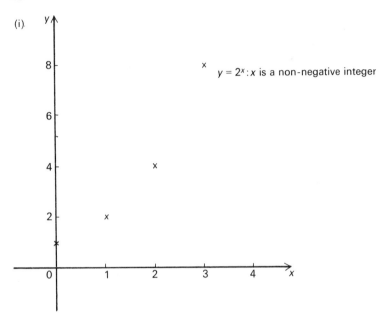

$y = 2^x : x$ is a non-negative integer

(ii)

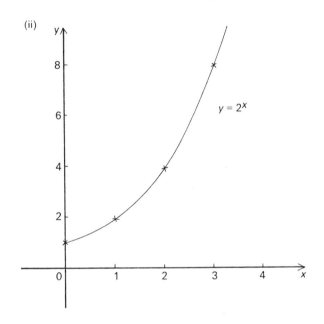

$y = 2^x$

Figure 6.13   Exponential growth.

In this case, because the weed is growing continuously, it is appropriate to extend the model to values of x other than integers; this amounts to joining the points by a smooth curve.

Another example of growth, but one in which it is not appropriate to join points by a smooth curve, is compound interest. Suppose £100 is invested at 8% interest, the interest to be paid at the end of each year and re-invested. Then after n completed years the amount £A of money invested would be given by the formula $A = 100 \times 1 \cdot 08^n$. The dotted line in figure 6.14 is the graph of the function $x \mapsto 100 \times 1 \cdot 08^x$, with domain the non-

negative numbers; but this is not a good model. The step-function shows the actual amount of money accumulated after x years, where x need not be an integer.

In general, a function of the form $x \mapsto a^x$ or $x \mapsto a^{-x}$ $(a > 1)$ is called an *exponential function*, the first modelling growth and the second modelling decay. The study of exponential functions is one of the major themes in calculus at the stage beyond sixteen. In the meantime, the calculator makes it easy for pupils to investigate numerically exponential functions such as those associated with continued doubling and with compound interest, which occur in a

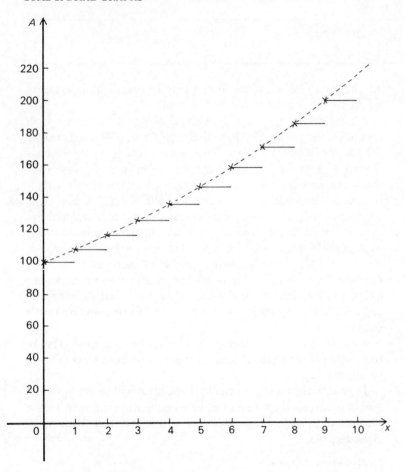

Figure 6.14   Investment growth with compound interest.

number of examples suitable at this stage. For example, the effect of the compounding of interest at more frequent intervals than once each year can be investigated.

6.7. Logarithms

The advent of the calculator has meant that the place of logarithms in the secondary mathematics curriculum is changing rapidly. Teachers who argue that their pupils will need logarithms for calculation in real life must think again; no one who has used a calculator will return willingly to logarithms. Some argue that calculators are too expensive for all pupils to have access to them, and that there are economic if not educational reasons for continuing to use logarithms; the authors believe that this argument will be short-lived, and that logarithms and slide rules will take their place alongside Napier's bones as interesting historical curiosities which aided calculation before better methods were developed.

In the sixth-form mathematics course, the natural logarithm will be needed and will be introduced either as the inverse of the exponential function or in terms of the area under the graph of $y = 1/x$. Teachers of pupils between eleven and sixteen need to decide whether there are reasons other than computational ones for teaching their pupils logarithms below the age of sixteen. The authors think the arguments for the retention of logarithms are weak, and that as sufficient calculators become available in schools for those pupils who do not have their own to have access to them, the teaching of logarithms before age sixteen should be discontinued.

7 What is Area?

7.1. An Approach

What is area? This is one of those deceptively simple questions which is much harder to answer than it looks. Some textbooks give a definition of the form "Area is the amount of surface covered" or "Area is the amount of space covered by a surface" but, as soon as we attempt to ask what the other words in these definitions mean, we see that they are not definitions at all.

A more helpful approach than attempting to define area, which is handled very well in *SMP Book B*, chapter 4, p. 36, is to consider the problem of how to compare two shapes in order to say which is the larger. It is necessary to remind pupils (because, of course, they will previously have met area in primary schools) precisely what it is that is supposed to be larger, for pupils are often unclear whether the perimeter or surface is meant. It may be useful to think in terms of paint required to cover the surface in conversations with pupils. Once it is established what is being investigated, it is clear that if the shapes are like A and B in figure 7.1 there is no problem, because one will fit inside the other; but if the shapes are like X and Y, a third shape Z is needed so that X and Z can first be compared, then Y and Z, and so X and Y can be compared with each other.

A convenient shape is then picked for Z, the only proviso being that copies of the shape Z must fit together without leaving holes (see figure 7.2).

In general the most convenient shape for Z will be the square. A grid of squares is then used to make an estimate of the area. This is illustrated in the following extract which is taken from *SMP Book B*, p. 43.

Measurement of area

To find the area of an irregular figure, it is convenient to use tracing paper. Either the outline of the figure can be traced and the tracing held over the top of the grid so that the squares can be counted, or the grid can be placed on tracing paper and held over the figure.

Figure 8 shows a shape drawn over the square grid. It is possible to count and *estimate* its area from the figure.

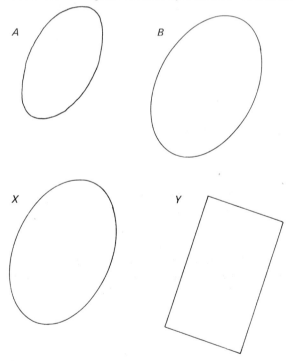

Figure 7.1

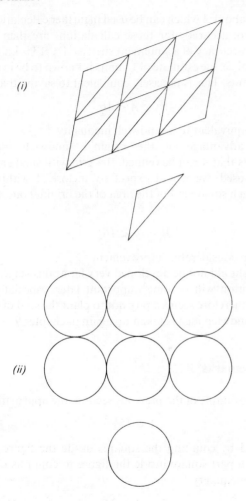

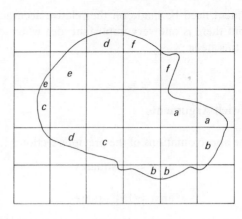

Fig. 8.

How many complete centimetre squares are there?

The complete squares have area	7
Two parts marked a	1
Three parts marked b	1
Two parts marked c	1
Two parts marked d	1
Two parts marked e	1
Two parts marked f	
together with the small unlettered parts	1
	13 squares

Other books make other suggestions about how to make the approximation. For example, some suggest first counting the number of complete squares inside the shape and then counting the number of part squares inside the shape, allowing each part square to count as one half of a complete square. In the extract shown above, there are 7 complete squares and 17 part squares, making a total of

$$7 + 17 \times \tfrac{1}{2} = 15\tfrac{1}{2} \text{ squares.}$$

Figure 7.2 (i) A convenient shape for Z; (ii) a bad choice for Z.

No comment need be made on the relative accuracy of these methods, but there is one very important idea which can be put forward at this stage.

7.2. Sandwich Arguments

While the approximations of the previous section

$$\text{area} \approx 13 \text{ squares}$$

and

$$\text{area} \approx 15\tfrac{1}{2} \text{ squares}$$

may be reasonably accurate statements, it is impossible to say how accurate they are. Neither is there any way of knowing whether or not 13 is a better approximation than $15\tfrac{1}{2}$. However, there is another statement which can be *guaranteed* to be correct. This is the statement that the area of the figure is sandwiched between an area of 7 whole squares and $24(=7+17)$ whole squares—in symbols

$$7 < A < 24$$

where A is the number of units of area covered by the figure. The essential difference between each of the statements

$$A \approx 13 \quad \text{and} \quad A \approx 15\tfrac{1}{2}$$

and the statement

$$7 < A < 24$$

is that while the first statements are vague, the second is precise. Without additional information there is no way of knowing how near A is to either 13 or to $15\tfrac{1}{2}$. On the other hand the second statement, $7 < A < 24$, is not an approximation at all. It gives information about A which can be used in further calculations, and exact limits of accuracy for those calculations are then known. Suppose the accuracy of a statement such as $A \approx 13$ is known and that, for instance, the estimate of 13 units is known to be in error by less than 3 units. This is precisely equivalent to saying that

$$10 < A < 16$$

that is, it is equivalent to a sandwich inequality.

Another advantage of the original sandwich inequality $7 < A < 24$ is that it can be refined. If a grid with smaller squares were to be used, we would expect to enclose A within closer bounds. If each square is $\tfrac{1}{4}$ of the area of the original one, then the result

$$9\tfrac{1}{4} < A < 16\tfrac{3}{4}$$

is obtained, a considerable improvement.

This idea should not be developed very far at this stage, but the sandwich notion will become important later, especially in integration. It therefore seems a pity not to plant the seed of the idea early. The sandwich idea is taken up again in chapter 9.

7.3. Two Remarks

(I) In the example of the previous section, the approximation

$$A \approx 15\tfrac{1}{2}$$

was obtained by counting the squares inside the figure and by allowing each part square inside the figure to count as one half-square. The inequality

$$7 < A < 24$$

was also obtained, and it will be noted that $15\tfrac{1}{2}$ is the average of 7 and 24, that is $15\tfrac{1}{2} = \tfrac{1}{2}(7+24)$.

That this is no coincidence may be seen by the following argument.

Let s be the number of complete squares inside the shape (see figure 7.3) and S the number of squares required to enclose the shape. Then the sandwich inequality states that

$$s < A < S$$

But the number of squares cut by the perimeter of the shape is $S-s$ and part of each of these squares lies inside the shape. Each of these $S-s$ cut-squares is taken to count one half-square towards the area.

Hence

$$A \approx s + \tfrac{1}{2}(S-s)$$

which simplifies to

$$A \approx \frac{s+S}{2}$$

It would be good practice to write down the sandwich inequality first and then to use it to write down an approximation for A. This would prepare the way for the development of the sandwich idea at a later stage.

(II) A different orientation of the figure, or a different position of the grid may very well give a different sandwich inequality, and so a different approximation for the area.

In figure 7.4 different positions of the square grid give different inequalities for the area A of the shaded square, namely,

$$1 < A < 9 \quad \text{and} \quad 0 < A < 4$$

and approximations

$$A \approx 5 \quad \text{and} \quad A \approx 2$$

then follow from these.

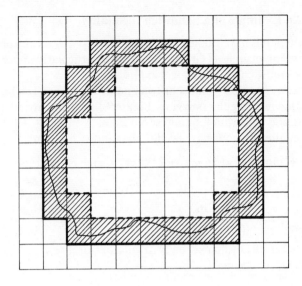

Figure 7.3   The sandwich inequality.

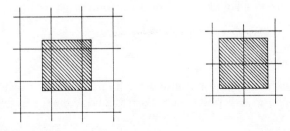

Figure 7.4   The effect of grid position on the approximation obtained from a sandwich inequality.

7.4. An Example of a Sandwich Inequality

When pupils have studied a little trigonometry, they can apply it to a revision of areas of circles and so use a particularly important type of sandwich inequality which arises.

A circle of radius 1 unit is drawn and its area is sandwiched by inner and outer regular polygons. Figure 7.5 shows inner and outer regular polygons with four and seven sides.

When the polygons have n sides, the sandwich formula

area of inner polygon < area of circle < area of outer polygon

becomes

$$n \sin \frac{360°}{2n} \cos \frac{360°}{2n} < \text{area of circle} < n \tan \frac{360°}{2n}$$

and the results, evaluated on a calculator, for $n = 4, 7, 360$ and 1800 respectively are

$$
\begin{aligned}
2 &\quad < \text{area of circle} < 4 \\
2 \cdot 736 &\quad < \text{area of circle} < 3 \cdot 371 \\
3 \cdot 1414 &\quad < \text{area of circle} < 3 \cdot 1417 \\
3 \cdot 141586 &< \text{area of circle} < 3 \cdot 141596
\end{aligned}
$$

It should be noted that for a calculator which gives nine decimal places, the sixth figure after the decimal point in the last line may be suspect.

7.5. Volume

A theory of volume may also be built up in a similar way to this theory of area, except that cubes correspond to the squares which

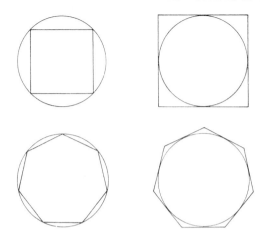

Figure 7.5   Approximations to the area of a circle.

were used before. However, it is interesting to reflect on two practical differences.

First, it is not possible in reality to put a network of cubes inside and outside a given container or shape whose volume is required. The exercise is entirely a mental one; that is, a mathematical model for volume has been made.

Secondly, volume is measured in the classroom by using a linear scale on a measuring cylinder of some kind. This draws attention to the fact that almost all physical quantities, for example, voltage, current, velocity and angle, are measured on a meter or some other linear scale. Area is a notable exception.

8 First Ideas of Speed and Gradient

8.1. First Experiences

Children's first experiences of *speeds* of movement are concerned with comparison of speeds. One running child overtakes another, one rhythm feels faster than another, one car gets away from traffic lights faster than another. No measurement is involved at this stage, and understanding of speed may not for some children be far enough advanced for its measurement to be meaningful until very late in the primary years. For the vast majority of children, their first acquaintance with the measurement of speed is concerned with the speed of cars. Both the speedometer of a car and the ubiquitous speed-limit signs serve to connect numbers with visual and bodily impressions of speed, and so to introduce the idea that speed is measurable.

Unfortunately, the speedometer of a car is almost the only device in everyday experience which measures a speed directly. The realization does not come easily, that the 30 which a speedometer registers at an instant means that if the car went on travelling *at the same speed* for an hour it would cover 30 miles. Nor is it immediately clear to pupils that, unless a speedometer is available, the only measure of how fast one is travelling is found by measuring the distance travelled in a particular time, and dividing the distance travelled by the time taken to give an *average speed* over that time.

8.2. Average Speed

An average speed must be measured over a particular period of time. When we say that the average speed of the London to Durham train is 120 kilometres per hour, it is implicit in the statement that the average is measured over the $3\frac{1}{2}$ hours of the journey. Over a particularly fast section of the journey, the average speed may be as great as 150 kilometres per hour. During the time of the stop at Darlington the average speed is zero.

There are many data available from which pupils can work out average speeds of trains and buses, and runners and swimmers. The calculation of average speeds from data within their experience helps pupils to grasp some important ideas about the measurement of speed:

(i) To measure speed, there has to be an interval of time over which the distance travelled is measured.

(ii) This process always leads to an *average* speed.

(iii) The units of average speed are units of distance divided by units of time (for instance, kilometres per hour or metres per second).

(iv) The average speed over an interval conceals variation in actual speed during that time.

(v) Motion at constant speed may provide a useful mathematical model for the real situation.

Figure 8.1(i) shows a distance-time graph which is a greatly simplified mathematical model of the journey of a London–Durham train.

The simple model of the straight-line graph needs careful discussion, so that pupils realize that *according to this model*, the train has travelled 120 km by the end of 1 hour, 240 km by the end of 2 hours, and so on. Hence they associate a straight-line distance-time graph with constant speed. Pupils may be encouraged to provide more-probable distance-time graphs than that of the straight-line model shown in figure 8.1, for instance by taking account of the stop at Darlington.

56

The discussion of such graphs in many texts does not bring out this modelling aspect of the graph. These books tend to give the impression that if the stop at Darlington on the Durham train is taken into account as in figure 8.1(ii), the train actually travels like that. Although the straight-line model with the stops shown is a good one, and is actually used by British Rail in their day-to-day timetabling, teachers should emphasize to pupils that the straight-line graph is only a simple approximate model which shows average speed very clearly.

Detailed discussion of such straight-line graphical models helps to bring out this fact that the interval of time over which an average speed is found may be very short. It is quite reasonable to say that the average speed of a train is 150 km/h for a period of 5 minutes; it means that in the 5 minutes in question the train travelled $12\frac{1}{2}$ km. To have an average speed of 150 km/h a train does not have to travel for 1 hour.

8.3. Gradient of a Straight-Line Distance-Time Graph

It is not a difficult idea that, for straight-line graphs of distance against time, the steeper graph represents the greater speed. It is important that the idea should be firmly linked with the *gradient* of the straight line, so that pupils implicitly realize that the gradient of the straight-line graph, which is measured by

$$\frac{\text{increase in } y}{\text{corresponding increase in } x},$$

numerically represents the constant speed which is shown by the graph. Of course, in measuring gradients from graphs, care must be taken to measure in the units which are used on the axes, as shown in figure 8.2(ii). This point is particularly important for distance-time graphs, where the scale for units of distance is unlikely to be related to the scale for units of time.

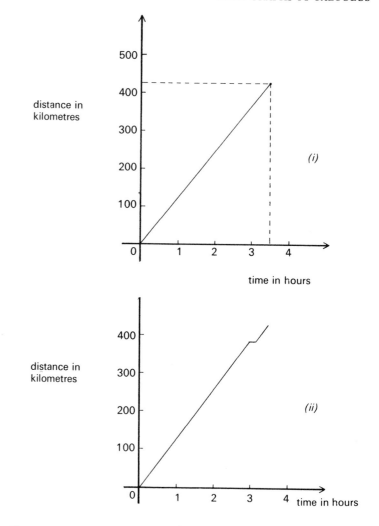

Figure 8.1 Distance-time graphs: (i) simplest model; (ii) model showing a stationary period.

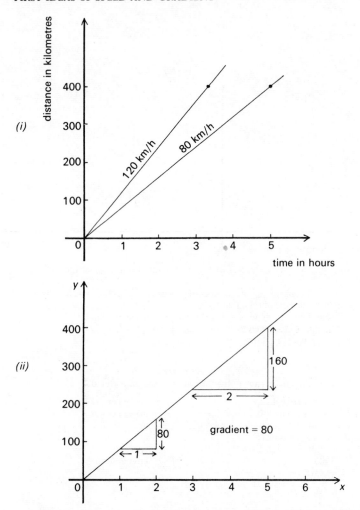

Figure 8.2   The gradient of a distance-time graph: (i) the steeper graph represents the greater speed; (ii) calculation of speed from gradient.

8.4. The Gradient of a Straight-Line Graph as a Rate

There are many other examples, as well as distance and time, where a real-life situation is usefully modelled by a straight-line graph, in such a way that the gradient of the graph is meaningful. In all these situations, the gradient of the straight-line graph represents a *rate*. Some examples are given below.

(i) Figure 8.3(i) shows the petrol consumption of a car. A straight line has been used as a model, and its gradient represents the *rate of consumption* of petrol, which is measured in *miles per gallon*.

(ii) Cloth is sold by the metre; a graph can be drawn of cost against length (figure 8.3(ii)). The marked price represents a *rate* of, for instance, £1·25 *per metre*. It is the gradient of this straight-line graph which represents the price rate of £1·25 per metre.

(iii) The *exchange rate* of francs against pounds is the gradient of the graph (figure 8.3(iii)) which shows how many francs the tourist will obtain for his pounds.

(iv) When cricketers measure the *rate of scoring* needed to win, they give it as, for instance, 7 runs per over. This is very clearly an *average* rate required over the remaining overs of the match, and fluctuates from over to over. In examples (ii) and (iii), however, although an average rate is used, it is a constant average rate.

These four examples call attention to the fact that in everyday life, a rate or (more properly) an average rate is not always measured with respect to time. Of course there are many examples of rates with respect to time, such as the rate of growth of a plant, or the rate of inflation, as well as our first example of speed.

Speed is not always clearly seen as a rate, but it is in fact the rate at which a moving body changes its distance from a fixed point with respect to time, and so is a *rate of change*. The units used for speed, such as *kilometres per hour*, are entirely comparable with other units for rates, such as *runs per over*, or *miles per gallon*.

The links between speed and other rates, and between rate and

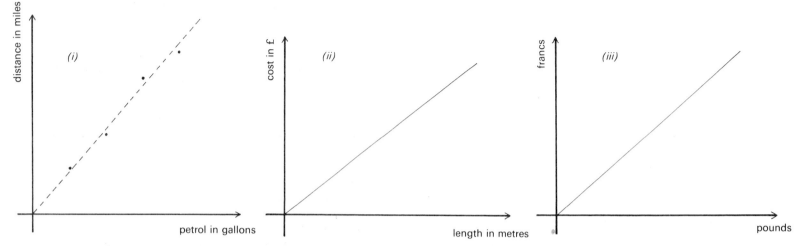

Figure 8.3   The gradient of a straight-line graph: (i) rate of consumption of petrol; (ii) price per unit of length; (iii) rate of exchange for foreign currency.

the gradient of a graph, need to be carefully made. The following extracts from *Modern Mathematics for Schools* (second edition) form a train of thought which needs careful development by the teacher if the pupils are to make the connections expected. The development from *rate of change* is particularly important

The costs of different numbers of a certain book are shown below.

Number of books		Number of pence in the cost
1	←——————————→	30
2	←——————————→	60
3	←——————————→	90
4	←——————————→	120
10	←——————————→	x
n	←——————————→	y

One-to-one correspondence. There is one, and only one, cost corresponding to a given number of books; and one, and only one, number of books corresponding to a given cost. So we say that there is a *one-to-one correspondence* between the number of books and the cost, as indicated by the arrows.

Rate. The *rate* giving the number of pence per book is the same for any pair of numbers in a row of the table.

From the first row we see that the *rate* is 30 pence per book.
The rate is also given by $\frac{60}{2}$, or $\frac{90}{3}$, or $\frac{120}{4}$, or $\frac{x}{10}$, or $\frac{y}{n}$.
(*MMS Book 3*, p. 167)

Exercise 2

1   Find the *rate* in each of the following, in the units stated:

a	8 oranges cost 24p;	pence per orange
b	20 bars of chocolate cost 90p;	pence per bar
c	273 units of electricity per week;	units per day
d	20 km in 4 hours;	km per hour
e	20 apples weigh 2 kg;	apples per kg
f	140 km take $2\frac{1}{2}$ hours;	km per hour

(*MMS Book 3*, p. 168)

Speed is rate of change of distance. When the speed is constant, the distance is proportional to the time and, as we saw in Chapter 2, the graph of a direct proportion relationship is a straight line.
(*MMS Book 3*, p. 206)

8.5. Gradient of a Road: a Red Herring

The usual first example of the gradient of a road or railway has been left until last, for the word *gradient* is not used in the same sense as it has been used above. The steep hill whose gradient is 1 in 6 is shown in figure 8.4. It is natural to measure the 6 units *along the*

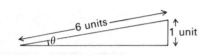

Figure 8.4   Gradient of a road.

road, rather than horizontally, so the gradient described by the road sign is sin θ, not tan θ. Moreover, a railway gradient post shows

$$\frac{1}{\sin \theta} \quad \text{or} \quad \text{cosec } \theta.$$

8.6. Gradients of Straight-Line Graphs

It is now an easy step to discuss the gradients of the graphs of straight-line functions, such as $x \mapsto 2x$. Pupils who have used straight-line graphs to model the situations above will realize that the gradient of the graph shows the rate of change, and so will realize that the study of the gradient of a straight-line graph such as that of the function $x \mapsto 2x$ gives important information about rates which can be applied in a variety of contexts. Pupils easily verify that the graph of the function $x \mapsto 2x$ has a gradient of 2.

Figure 8.5   Gradient of a railway line.

Pupils will also have drawn graphs such as that of the function $x \mapsto -2x$ (figure 8.6(ii)). They will see that to an increase in x there corresponds a decrease, or a negative increase, in y. Thus the definition of the gradient of a straight line,

$$\frac{\text{increase in } y}{\text{corresponding increase in } x}$$

inevitably attaches a negative gradient to such a straight line.

Similarly, the graph of the function $x \mapsto mx + c$ has a gradient of m. However, this last statement represents a considerable step in abstraction from the previous one, for now a general statement about the whole class of straight-line functions is made, and the teacher should not take this last step until he is sure his pupils are ready for it.

8.7. A Change of Wording

One further point needs to be made; it concerns the nature of the words *distance* and *speed*. It is unfortunate that these words, which are used so much in everyday speech and thought, are not

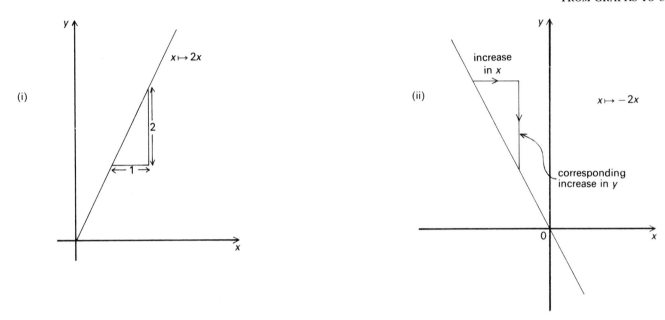

Figure 8.6   (i) A positive gradient; (ii) a negative gradient.

considered by mathematicians to be sufficiently precise. Gradients of straight-line graphs may be either positive or negative, but average speeds are always thought of as positive. The word *velocity* is used when the *direction* of a speed is taken into account, so velocity is allowed to be negative. Hence it is *average velocity* which corresponds to the gradient of the straight-line graph. In a similar way the *distance* between two points is always positive, while when mathematicians wish to allow for the possibility of negative distance they use the word *displacement*.

These "official" words will be used in those remaining parts of the book which use the ideas of motion.

The ideas of this chapter are developed in chapter 12.

9 Numbers

9.1. The Need for Real Numbers in Graphical Work

When a pupil is asked to draw the graph of a function such as $x \mapsto x^2$ and to join the small number of points he has plotted to form a curve, there is an implicit assumption that *each* point of the x-axis represents a number and that *each* point of the y-axis also represents a number.

Pupils might then be asked to read off from the graph of $x \mapsto x^2$ an approximation to the positive number whose square is 20. This task carries the implicit assumption that there is such a number,

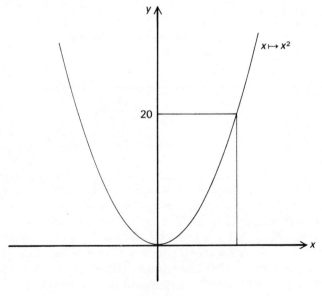

Figure 9.1

and the pupil is usually (and rightly) expected to accept this assumption in good faith without even realizing that it is an assumption.

If, instead, a pupil attempts to find $\sqrt{20}$ using a calculator, the calculator may show that

$$\sqrt{20} = 4\cdot47213595$$

but when the number on the right-hand side is squared it is found not to be exactly equal to 20.* Indeed, none of the successive approximations which a calculator might produce,

$$4\cdot4, \ 4\cdot47, \ 4\cdot472, \ 4\cdot4721 \text{ and so on,}$$

has a square which is exactly 20, although the sequence has a *limit* whose square is exactly 20. This concept of a limit, which will be necessary in the later study of integration and differentiation, will involve pupils in an intuitive appreciation of the complete system of real numbers.

This chapter is devoted to a discussion of a way in which this intuitive appreciation of real numbers may develop in children before the age of sixteen by using the interplay between numbers and their representation on the real number-line; that is, by using the interplay between arithmetical and geometrical thinking about numbers.

Many of the ideas are subtle and delicate. The teacher will be introducing them implicitly in discussion and by assumption, rather than by formal exposition, over a period of some years. The

---

* Care is needed here for a calculator may appear to show that $(4\cdot47213595)^2 = 20$. However, it is clear that in an exact calculation there will be a 5 in the sixteenth place after the decimal point of the product.

development of pupils' concepts of number is one of the most important tasks in mathematics, and this chapter is therefore addressed to the teacher, so that he may examine the development of the number concept as it is needed for later work in calculus. The level of exposition is often more sophisticated than that which would be suitable for pupils, who may take for granted much of what is explicitly stated here.

9.2. Early Stages

By the age of eleven, most children have absorbed the whole numbers into their thinking. They have met the number-line and they see the whole numbers as attached to equally spaced points on

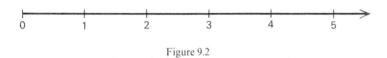

Figure 9.2

the number-line with zero as the starting point on the line. They also know that the bigger the number, the further to the right it is on the number-line.

They are also familiar with the denary way of writing whole numbers, using hundreds, tens and units, and can carry out, to varying extents, procedures for adding, subtracting, multiplying and dividing whole numbers. Pupils may not be aware how efficient the denary system of writing numbers is compared with, say, the Roman system. Not only are the denary procedures for the four rules much simpler than corresponding procedures would be in the Roman system, but the denary system gives such a simple method for deciding which is the larger of two numbers that we take the method for granted, automatically comparing digits of the two numbers.

The interaction of three ideas, the number itself, its representation on the number-line, and its written representation in the denary system for the purposes of calculation and comparison, forms the theme of this chapter.

9.3. Fractions and Decimals on the Number-Line

Most pupils know before the age of eleven how some simple fractions such as $\frac{3}{4}$ or $1\frac{1}{2}$ and some decimals can be represented on the number-line, using different scales as convenient (see figure 9.3).

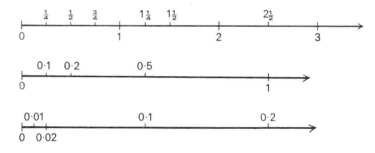

Figure 9.3

The ruler-and-compass construction which enables a line-segment to be divided into a number of equal parts is a most useful aid in enabling pupils to visualize the position of fractional points on the number-line. To find points on the number-line corresponding to $\frac{1}{7}, \frac{2}{7}, \ldots, \frac{6}{7}$, for instance (figure 9.4), a line is drawn through O at an angle to the number-line, and seven equal lengths are stepped off along it. Parallels are then drawn to the line joining P to the point 1 of the number-line.

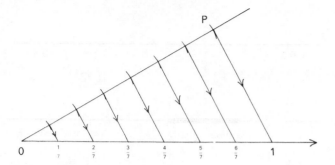

Figure 9.4   Geometrical construction for positioning fractional points on the number-line.

Thus, fractions are easily made to correspond to points of the number-line. Fractions are also comparatively easily added, subtracted, multiplied and divided by well-known procedures. However, it is not easy to tell at a glance whether, for instance, $\frac{13}{21}$ is greater than $\frac{5}{8}$. When two fractions such as these are to be compared, it is necessary to replace them both by equivalent fractions with a common denominator, so that for example $\frac{5}{8} > \frac{13}{21}$, since $\frac{5}{8} = \frac{105}{168}$ and $\frac{13}{21} = \frac{104}{168}$. The pupil will not be able actually to mark these points on a number-line, but we expect that he probably will have some picture such as that of figure 9.5 in his imagination.

Figure 9.5

A correspondence has now been set up between some arithmetical ideas and some geometrical ideas. These ideas are the development from whole numbers to fractions, and the develop-ment from a number-line with equally spaced points marked to a number-line with fractional points marked.

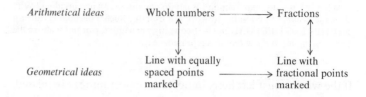

As well as knowing that fractions may be marked on the number-line and may be written using a pair of whole numbers such as $\frac{3}{4}$, many primary-school children know that $\frac{3}{4}$ may also be written as the decimal 0·75. Indeed they may have met the decimal form first. The decimal fractions which a pupil knows at this stage are very easily ordered on the number-line, although some pupils may, for a time, be deceived by the digits into thinking that, for instance, 0·075 is a larger number than 0·13. It is essential for the eventual understanding of the real-number system that pupils should understand that the decimal notation to which they are accustomed merely gives another way of writing some fractions; 0·13 is only another way of writing $\frac{1}{10} + \frac{3}{100}$ or $\frac{13}{100}$. In the same way, 0·25 is another way of writing $\frac{25}{100}$, which is that very familiar fraction $\frac{1}{4}$. Unfortunately, although to every terminating decimal there corresponds a fraction, it is *not* true that to every fraction there corresponds a terminating decimal. The attempt to convert fractions to decimals leads to the exploration of recurring de-cimals.

9.4. Recurring Decimals on the Number-Line

When $\frac{1}{3}$ is converted by division into a decimal, there is at every stage a remainder. It is usual practice, as in the quotation below from *Maths Today*, to introduce recurring decimals at this point (*Maths Today, Book 1*, pp. 159–60).

> What is $\frac{1}{3}$ as a decimal fraction? What do you discover when dividing? Why does the decimal fraction fail to work out exactly? Such a decimal is called a RECURRING DECIMAL and we frequently put a full stop or point above the recurring figure to show that it is repeated—e.g.,
>
> $$\frac{1}{3} = 0\cdot\dot{3} = 0\cdot33333\ldots$$

If the work is just left here, important opportunities are missed. Pupils can mark a point which represents $\frac{1}{3}$ on the number-line by a ruler-and-compass construction. They can also mark on the number-line the first few decimal approximations

$$0\cdot3, 0\cdot33, 0\cdot333,$$

to the fraction $\frac{1}{3}$.

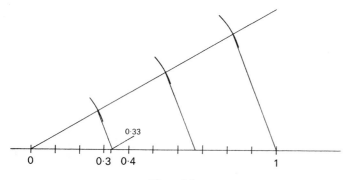

Figure 9.6

In practice, the point on the number-line representing $0\cdot333$ is indistinguishable from that representing $\frac{1}{3}$; however, because $3 \times 0\cdot333 = 0\cdot999$, so that $0\cdot333$ is not equal to $\frac{1}{3}$, and similarly for each of the approximations. Thus, none of the points which represent $0\cdot3, 0\cdot33, 0\cdot333, \ldots$ should fall *exactly* on the point which represents $\frac{1}{3}$.

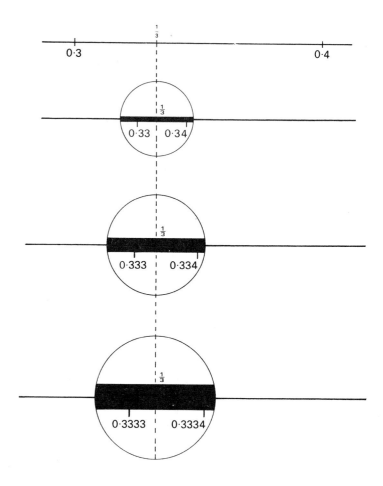

Figure 9.7 Successive decimal approximations to one third on the number-line.

It is well worth discussing the sequence of sandwiching inequalities which occur at the successive stages of the division which converts $\frac{1}{3}$ to a decimal. First

$$0\cdot3 < \tfrac{1}{3} < 0\cdot4$$

since, multiplying by three, $3 \times 0\cdot3 < 1$, but $1 < 3 \times 0\cdot4$. Hence

$$0\cdot3 \quad < \tfrac{1}{3} < 0\cdot4$$
$$0\cdot33 \quad < \tfrac{1}{3} < 0\cdot34$$
$$0\cdot333 \quad < \tfrac{1}{3} < 0\cdot334$$
$$0\cdot3333 < \tfrac{1}{3} < 0\cdot3334$$

and so on. Figure 9.7 illustrates these inequalities in terms of successive magnifications of a ruler graduated in tenths, hundredths, thousandths, etc., of a unit.

The width of the sandwich inequality decreases at each step by a factor of ten:

$$0\cdot3 < \tfrac{1}{3} < 0\cdot4$$
$$0\cdot1$$

$$0\cdot33 < \tfrac{1}{3} < 0\cdot34$$
$$0\cdot01$$

so that although the decimal graduation points on the number-line become indefinitely close together, none of them ever falls exactly on the point which corresponds to $\frac{1}{3}$. The explicit discussion of this point may help pupils to extend their ideas about number.

But if a number-line which is graduated in thirds, ninths, etc., of a unit is taken instead of one which is graduated in tenths,

hundredths, etc., then, working in base three instead of base ten, it is found that

$$\tfrac{1}{3} = 0\cdot1 \text{ (base three)}.$$

Similarly the proper fraction p/q is written in base q as $0\cdot p$. Thus a fractional number always has a terminating representation in some number-base, even though its decimal (base ten) representation may not terminate. Whichever base is chosen, however, the majority of fractional numbers have recurring rather than terminating representations.

Clearly, each terminating decimal is equivalent to a fraction; for instance, $0\cdot23 = \frac{23}{100}$. It will be shown in section 9.8 that each recurring decimal is equivalent to a fraction; for instance $0\cdot1\dot{5} = \frac{5}{33}$. It will be assumed that, conversely, each fraction may be written in base ten as either a terminating or a recurring decimal. Hence the previous correspondence between arithmetical and geometrical ideas may be extended to the following:

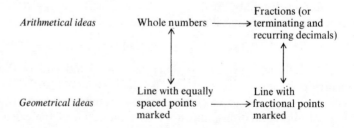

When directed numbers are introduced, the number-line needs to be extended indefinitely in the negative as well as the positive direction, so that it can represent positive and negative whole numbers and fractions. At this time, official mathematical vocabulary can be introduced: the positive and negative whole numbers are the *integers*, and the positive and negative whole numbers and fractions together make up the *rational numbers*. The correspondence now contains three sets of ideas:

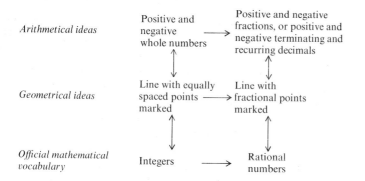

9.5. Calculating with Recurring Decimals

The procedures which children have learned for calculating with terminating decimals break down for decimals which do not terminate. For example, it is not possible to calculate directly

$$0.33333\ldots\ldots \times 0.142857142857\ldots\ldots$$

because it is not possible to find "the right-hand end of the recurring decimal". All that can be done is to cut short the recurring decimals, to calculate with the resulting terminating decimal approximations, and hope that the result of the calculation is a reasonable approximation to the answer.

Exact calculation of the product of the two recurring decimals above is possible by converting them to fractions, carrying out the multiplication and then reconverting to a decimal. This gives

$$\tfrac{1}{3} \times \tfrac{1}{7} = \tfrac{1}{21} = 0.047619047619047619\ldots\ldots$$

The change from a fractional representation of a rational number to a decimal representation has resulted in the loss of

procedures for exact calculation. This might be considered as the price paid for the beauty of the decimal system in which the relative sizes of any two numbers may be distinguished by inspection.

Pupils who have begun to explore fractions on the number-line probably think that to every point of the number-line there corresponds a number of a type they know: in other words, a rational number. At this stage, it is difficult not to reinforce the belief that every point on the number-line corresponds to a rational number, because of the very necessary emphasis which must be placed on interpolation from graphs. From the graph of $x \mapsto x^2$, a pupil finds that (as nearly as he can tell) $\sqrt{20} = 4.5$. He should also be encouraged to verify that $(4.5)^2 = 20.25$, so that his result, although near, is too big: $\sqrt{20} < 4.5$. With a sharper pencil, a larger scale and a good deal of luck he may obtain the approximation 4.47 for $\sqrt{20}$. But $(4.47)^2 = 19.9809$, so $4.47 < \sqrt{20} < 4.5$. It is likely that pupils will draw from this the belief that if only they could be accurate enough, or if they had a calculator with enough decimal places, they could find a decimal whose square is exactly 20.

It is one of the most remarkable discoveries of Greek mathematics, and still comes as a great shock to many pupils today, that there is no rational number whose square is exactly 20. But much further preparation is needed before pupils will appreciate the significance of this fact.

9.6. The Sandwiching Process and Measurement

A further step in the argument comes from the combination of sandwich inequalities with ideas derived from practical measurement. No measurement made with a ruler or other measuring instrument is ever exact; measurements are made "to the nearest...". The statement that the length of the room is 4·27 m must be taken to mean that it is in the range from 4·265 m to 4·275 m. It has been (presumably) measured to the nearest centimetre, so that the actual measurement is sandwiched in an interval of length 1 cm (or 0·01 m).

$$\underbrace{4\cdot265 \leqslant l \leqslant 4\cdot275}_{0\cdot01}$$

Similarly, when a pupil says that, from his graph, $\sqrt{20}$ is approximately 4·5, he probably means that the point is nearer to 4·5 than to 4·4 or 4·6; for him

$$\underbrace{4\cdot45 \leqslant \sqrt{20} \leqslant 4\cdot55}_{0\cdot1}$$

It is important for the teacher to realize that the graduation marks on measuring instruments are placed at points representing rational numbers, so that every measurement is always sand-wiched by a pair of rational numbers. In the example of the length of the room, the precise length is not known: it is only known that the length is sandwiched between the rational numbers 4·265 and 4·275.

The previous sandwiching example of decimal approximations to $\frac{1}{3}$ contains an additional feature: each inequality sandwiches $\frac{1}{3}$ between rational numbers such as 0·33 and 0·34, or 0·3333 and 0·3334, but the sandwich inequalities also lead to intervals of decreasing length, each interval nested within the previous one; thus $\frac{1}{3}$ can be enclosed in as short an interval as we please. This idea

of enclosing a number in a sequence of sandwich inequalities whose width can be indefinitely decreased (figure 9.8) is of utmost importance when moving from the rational numbers to the irrational numbers.

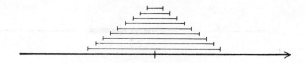

Figure 9.8   Successive approximations to a value for a point x on a number-line.

9.7. Describing Points on the Number-Line

The decimal number system provides a way of labelling *every* point on the number-line, not only those which correspond to terminating decimals. A point marked on the number-line either falls on an integer point, or it falls between two integers. The number corresponding to the point labelled x in figure 9.9 lies between 2 and 3, so that $2 \leqslant x \leqslant 3$, and the decimal representation of the number either starts 2·, or is exactly 3. Next, tenths of a unit are used; so that x satisfies

$$2\cdot7 \leqslant x \leqslant 2\cdot8$$

Using hundredths of a unit

$$2\cdot74 \leqslant x \leqslant 2\cdot75$$

It may happen that this process terminates at some stage, so that, for instance, when thousandths of a unit are used, $x = 2\cdot743$. However, it is much more likely that the process never terminates, so that the number x can only be described as a decimal by the sequence of nested intervals within which it is sandwiched, as shown on page 68.

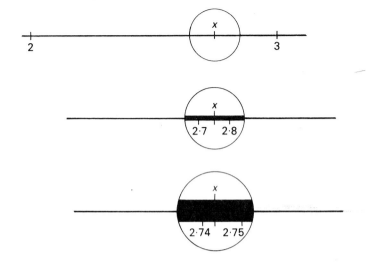

Figure 9.9   Successive approximations to a value for a point x on a number-line.

Sandwich inequality	Length of interval
$2 \leqslant x \leqslant 3$	1
$2\cdot7 \leqslant x \leqslant 2\cdot8$	0·1
$2\cdot74 \leqslant x \leqslant 2\cdot75$	0·01
$2\cdot742 \leqslant x \leqslant 2\cdot743$	0·001
$2\cdot7429 \leqslant x \leqslant 2\cdot7430$	0·0001

and so on.

Pupils can be shown how this point is represented by

$$2\cdot7429\ldots\ldots$$

where the dots indicate that further steps in the sandwiching process have not yet been described. If the decimal corresponding to the point on the number-line neither terminates nor recurs, then the number is not a rational number, since all rational numbers have terminating or recurring decimal expressions. These num-

bers, decimals which neither terminate nor recur, are *irrational numbers*. The rational and irrational numbers together make up the *real* numbers.

Two assumptions are implicit in the above description, and the intention is that pupils should informally take them for granted in their own thinking. If they do so, they will have nothing to unlearn later, and they will be well prepared for a deeper understanding of the real numbers when they are older. The assumptions are:

(i) Every point of the number-line corresponds to a real number.

(ii) The position of a given point of the number-line can be described by a sandwiching process, and the corresponding real number represented by a decimal.

In this book we have called this second assumption the *sandwich assumption*.

At a later stage in their mathematical development, the most-able students will realize that the second assumption is the "Chinese Box Theorem", which states that if we have a sequence of nested closed intervals on the real number-line whose lengths tend to zero, then there is exactly one real number which is common to all the intervals; that is, every sequence of nested closed intervals converges to a number and not to a gap between numbers. Of course the *real number* to which the sequence of nested intervals converges may be either a rational number or an irrational number.

9.8.   Changing Recurring Decimals to Fractions

The links between rational numbers and terminating or recurring decimals are not complete until pupils realize that *every* recurring decimal, as well as every terminating decimal, corresponds to a rational number.

The following method of showing how a recurring decimal can

be converted to a fraction is suitable for discussion with abler pupils, but it depends on assumptions about the convergence of infinite series which will not be made explicit at this stage. The method is illustrated for $0.1\overline{2}\overline{3}$.

$$x = \quad 0.1\dot{2}\dot{3}$$

$$\Rightarrow 1000x = 123.1\dot{2}\dot{3}$$

$$\Rightarrow \quad 999x = 123$$

$$\Rightarrow \quad\quad x = \tfrac{123}{999}$$

$$= \tfrac{41}{333}$$

The correspondence which was introduced earlier, between arithmetical and geometrical ideas and the official mathematical language, can now be completed:

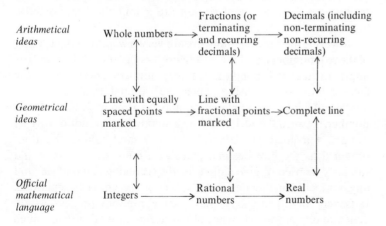

The third line of the table, which gives the official mathematical names for the different set of numbers, can be introduced as the ideas are understood.

9.9. Calculation with Real Numbers

Although pairs of irrational numbers are easily ordered, irrational numbers, like recurring decimals, are extremely awkward for purposes of calculation. Whenever irrational numbers occur they can always be sandwiched between rational numbers. Calculations are always carried out using the rational approximations.

For instance, if two positive real numbers r and s are sandwiched between positive terminating decimals a, b and c, d respectively, so that

$$a \leqslant r \leqslant b$$

and

$$c \leqslant s \leqslant d$$

then

$$a+c \leqslant r+s \leqslant b+d$$

and

$$ac \leqslant rs \leqslant bd$$

Only minor adjustments are needed when the real numbers concerned are not positive. Moreover, these sandwich inequalities can always be made as thin as we please by taking decimal approximations which are close enough to r and s.

This is the basis of all numerical calculation with irrational numbers, whether done on paper or using a calculator, a computer or logarithm tables. Mathematical tables are simply dictionaries which give terminating decimal approximations for numbers such as $\log 2$, $\sin 35°$ and so on. Calculators give similar rational approximations to real numbers. Once these rational approximations have been found, then the calculation is carried out entirely in rational numbers according to the usual procedures, the sandwich inequalities leading to a guarantee that the resulting rational number will be fairly close to the required real number.

Thus, for everyday purposes of calculation, rational numbers rather than real numbers are used. Mathematically, however, it is important that the most-able pupils should realize that irrational numbers are part of the theoretical construction of the number system.

9.10. The Introduction of Irrational Numbers in Texts

In most texts, irrational numbers are first encountered in connection with Pythagoras' Theorem and the need for square roots. A typical treatment is that of the Scottish Mathematics Group shown below (*Modern Mathematics for Schools, Book 4*, p. 19):

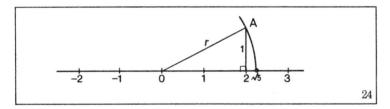

24

From figure 24, using Pythagoras' theorem,

$$r^2 = 2^2 + 1^2 = 5$$

Hence $r = \sqrt{5} = 2 \cdot 236 \ldots$, a number which cannot be expressed as a ratio of two integers or as a decimal. Therefore $\sqrt{5}$ does not belong to Q.

$\sqrt{5}$ is called an *irrational* number. We can find its approximate position on the number line by drawing an arc of a circle with centre O and radius OA as shown.

This is a good opportunity for raising several points in class discussion. First, on the real number-line which the pupils visualize, the *exact* position of the point representing $\sqrt{5}$ can be constructed by the method described. Secondly, the statement $r = \sqrt{5} = 2 \cdot 236 \ldots$ can usefully be examined by the sandwich method described above

Sandwich inequality	Length of interval
$2 \quad \leqslant \sqrt{5} \leqslant 3$	1
$2 \cdot 2 \quad \leqslant \sqrt{5} \leqslant 2 \cdot 3$	0·1
$2 \cdot 23 \quad \leqslant \sqrt{5} \leqslant 2 \cdot 24$	0·01
$2 \cdot 236 \leqslant \sqrt{5} \leqslant 2 \cdot 237$	0·001

At this stage, pupils may begin to realize intuitively why the sandwiching process can never end, for to obtain a terminating decimal whose square is exactly $5 \cdot 000 \ldots 0$, the last digit would have to be 0, and so would the digit before, and so on. Thus, discussion of the sandwiching process helps to build up the realization that non-terminating non-recurring decimals, or irrational numbers, do actually turn up in mathematics. Apart from the square roots, other irrational numbers which pupils are likely to meet before the age of sixteen are π and the trigonometric functions.

However, the rational numbers are very few among the totality of the real numbers, and the vast majority of points of the number-line do in fact correspond to irrational numbers. This fact is on the face of it most surprising, when the rational numbers are so familiar. An informal explanation may be given as follows. A real number between 0 and 1 could be generated in a random way by using a ten-sided die labelled $0, 1, \ldots 9$, and taking the digit obtained as the first decimal place of a number. The die could similarly be used to give a digit for the second decimal place, and any number of further decimal places could be similarly generated. It is very highly unlikely that such a random process would generate one of the two types of non-terminating decimals which correspond to rational numbers: those such as $0 \cdot 342134213421 \ldots$ in which there is *always* a cyclic repetition, and those such as $0 \cdot 250000000 \ldots$ which correspond to terminating decimals. Thus, it appears probable that comparatively very few real numbers are rational.

9.11. Proofs of Irrationality

Able pupils will be interested to see how the fact that a number such as $\sqrt{5}$ is irrational can be established. All such arguments are proofs by contradiction, a method which able pupils should meet before they are sixteen.

The proof that $\sqrt{5}$ is irrational begins by supposing, on the contrary, that $\sqrt{5}$ is a rational number. Hence there are integers p and q such that

$$\frac{p}{q} = \sqrt{5}$$

and so

$$p^2 = 5q^2.$$

Because q^2 is a perfect square, it has an even number of prime factors. Thus $5q^2$ has an odd number of prime factors. But $5q^2 = p^2$ and therefore p^2 must have an odd number of prime factors. But this contradicts the fact that p^2 is a perfect square. Hence $\sqrt{5}$ is not a rational number.

This proof clearly extends to a proof that the square root of every prime number is irrational.

It is worth noticing that the above proof is independent of the number base chosen to represent p and q. This emphasizes the fact that an irrational number cannot be written as a fraction in *any* number base, a point about which pupils sometimes have doubts. By contrast, the expansion of a rational number always terminates in *some* base, as was shown in section 9.4.

9.12. Recommendations

It is suggested that the following ideas should form the goal of work on the real numbers with able pupils.

1. Every point on the number-line corresponds to a real number and, conversely, every real number corresponds to a point on the number-line.
2. To every fraction there corresponds a terminating or recurring decimal, and conversely, to every terminating or recurring decimal there corresponds a fraction.
3. Every real number, whether rational or irrational, can be approximated to within any required degree of accuracy using terminating decimals.
4. Calculations can only be carried out by the procedures for terminating decimals.

Finally, the concept of real numbers is very closely bound up with the related idea of a limit, which is discussed in the next chapter.

10 The Idea of a Limit

10.1. Strategy

Although the idea of a limit, and the notation for limits, lie at the heart of the differential calculus, they receive little attention in the introduction to differentiation in any of the texts reviewed. This is not because ideas about limits have been growing steadily throughout the secondary course—far from it. In fact, it is usual for the idea of a limit to be met for the first time in the most difficult of all possible circumstances: the limits commonly used in differentiation, which are limits of fractions where both the numerator and the denominator tend to zero. This is conceptually the most baffling situation in which to grasp the idea of a limit. It is suggested in this chapter that there are many fairly simple mathematical situations in which pupils can gain informal experience of limits from very early in the secondary school. If they do this, they will find the limits used in differentiation easier to understand, and progress will be correspondingly greater.

It is not suggested that a formal treatment of limits should form part of the work done by secondary pupils; that must properly be deferred for higher education. However, some reference to limits is essential to any work on differentiation and is also needed for the study of infinite geometric and other series at the next stage of education.

It is extremely difficult to convey in print the delicacy of touch which is necessary. The work described subsequently in this chapter is not suitable for conventional teaching and testing, and there may be little or no written output by the pupil. The aim is to encourage ideas to grow gradually, and there need be no attempt in the early years to draw things together. Many of the ideas suggested are suitable either for group working or for individual worksheets. Discussion between pupils will make an important contribution to the work.

10.2. First Ideas

In the primary school, children meet many situations in which a process is repeated again and again, and the same process could be repeated indefinitely. Many of these repetitive processes are concerned with sequences.

(i) Peter (aged 9) said "Tie a knot in your handkerchief to remind you. And another to remind you what that's for. And another. And another. And...."

(ii) A familiar exercise is "Give the next three terms of the sequences

$$1, 3, 7, 13, \ldots.$$
$$2, 3, 5, 8, 12, \ldots."$$

(iii) Squares are often made with Cuisenaire rods. Children explore how many units are needed to turn each square into the next one (figure 10.1).

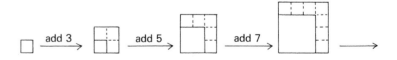

Figure 10.1   Construction of squares with Cuisenaire rods.

72

(iv) Repeated doubling produces a sequence whose terms grow very rapidly: 1, 2, 4, 8, 16, 32, 64, 128, 256, 512, 1024, . . .

From these experiences, children gain the idea that many mathematical processes could be repeated indefinitely, or as they say, "for ever". Peter's enjoyment came from his vision of knotted handkerchiefs receding into the dim distance. But, at this stage, most of the work is done with whole numbers, so that the terms of the sequences are likely to grow beyond all bounds. Ideas about limits begin to develop when situations can be explored in which a sequence "settles down" or converges. This may initially be more vivid in geometrical rather than arithmetical contexts.

10.3. A Geometrical Introduction to Convergent Sequences

(i) A square of side 1 dm is drawn, and rectangles and squares are alternately built on to it, as shown in figure 10.2. Each shape added has an area which is one half of that added previously. What happens to the total area?

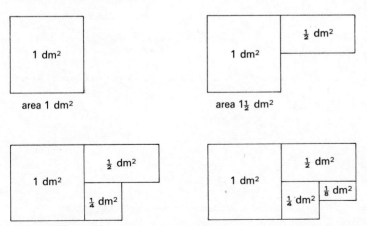

Figure 10.2 Geometrical introduction to convergent sequences.

We return to this example to discuss its mathematical implications in section 10.5.

(ii) A variation on this situation is obtained by rearranging the squares and rectangles into a spiral, as shown in figure 10.3. Pupils can investigate to which point the spiral converges.

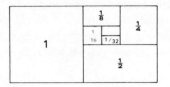

Figure 10.3

(iii) Curve stitching is an activity which many pupils will have met in the primary school. Two intersecting lines are taken and equal intervals are marked off from the point of intersection; the

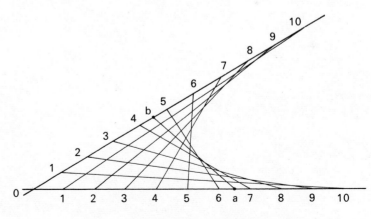

Figure 10.4   Curve stitching.

points on each line are numbered as shown in figure 10.4, the point 1 is joined to 10, 2 to 9 and so on. The lines appear to form a curve. This is illusory, but better and better approximations may be obtained by inserting more and more lines, using the rule $a + b = 11$ for deciding which points should be joined; a and b may be fractional or negative.

(iv) Pursuit curves give another method of approximating to curves by using small line segments. A dog D is chasing a rabbit R. The rabbit runs along a straight line at 1 m/s. The dog can run at 1·5 m/s and always aims directly towards the rabbit.

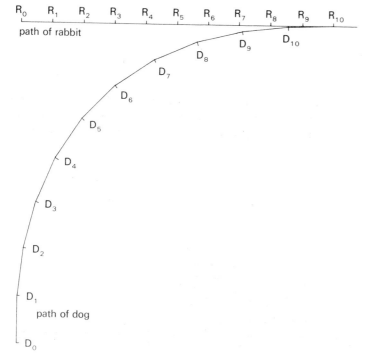

Figure 10.5   Pursuit curve: a dog chasing a rabbit.

Positions of the rabbit are drawn at $R_0, R_1, \ldots, R_{10}$, each 1 unit apart. Each part of the dog's path is 1·5 units long and $D_0 D_1$ is directed towards R_0, $D_1 D_2$ towards R_1, $D_2 D_3$ towards R_2 and so on. The dog catches the rabbit after about 12 seconds. By taking short enough time intervals, the path drawn can be made as close to the actual path of the dog as we please.

(v) Another example of a similar type concerns four cannibalistic beetles. These beetles, A, B, C and D start at the corners of a square. A wants to eat B, B wants to eat C, C wants to eat D, and D wants to eat A. All the beetles walk at the same speed, and the path of each beetle is aimed directly towards the beetle it is chasing.

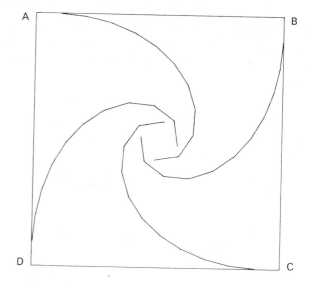

Figure 10.6   Pursuit curve: four cannibalistic beetles.

Step-by-step approximations to their paths are shown in figure 10.6. The example breaks down near the point at the centre of the

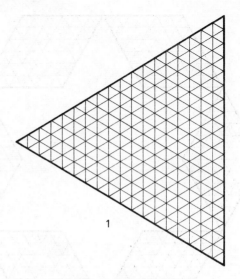

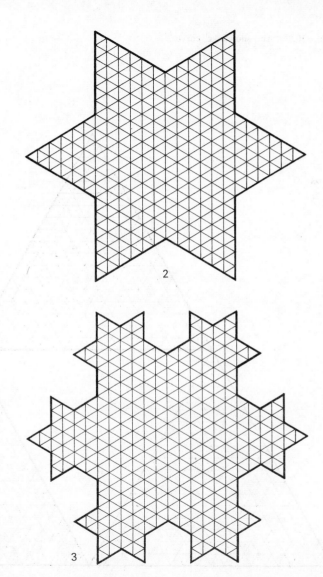

Figure 10.7 "Snowflake" curve.

spirals, but once again intuition suggests that the use of shorter steps would have given a closer approximation to the actual paths.

It is interesting that in the last two examples we are, in effect, solving differential equations by step-by-step methods. This idea is introduced in section 16.4

(vi) The last geometrical example is of the snowflake curve, and returns to the sandwiching theme. To construct the curve, an equilateral triangle is drawn and each side is divided into three equal parts. An equilateral triangle is constructed on the middle third, as shown in figure 10.7, and the process of constructing equilateral triangles on the middle third of each line is repeated indefinitely.

It is clear that both the area and the perimeter of the snowflake curve increase at each step. Construction of the first few approxi-

Figure 10.8 "Anti-snowflake" curve.

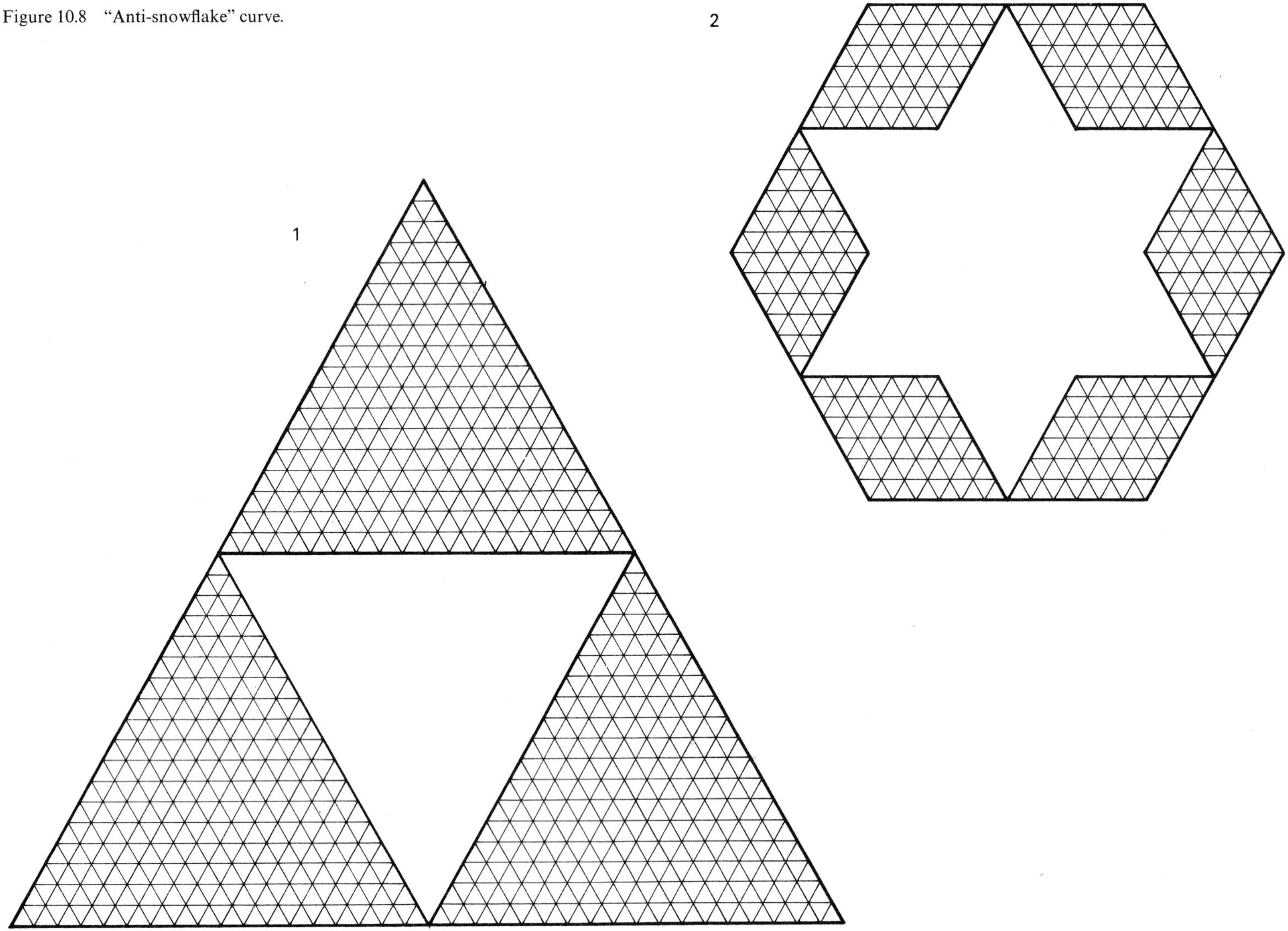

3

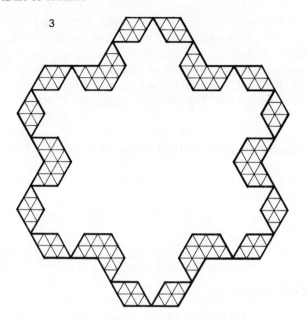

4

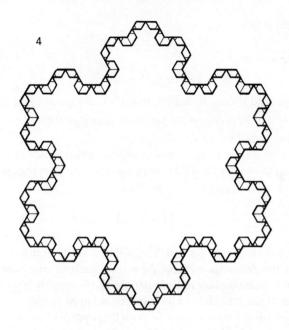

mations both to the snowflake curve, and to the "anti-snowflake" curve which is obtained by inscribing the original equilateral triangle in a larger one, and then at each step drawing inward-facing equilateral triangles on the two outer thirds of each line (figure 10.8) will convince pupils that the area and perimeter of the snowflake curve behave differently. The area is sandwiched between the areas of the snowflake and anti-snowflake curves (figure 10.8). The perimeter of the snowflake, however, is multi-plied by $\frac{4}{3}$ at each step, as the effect of the construction at each step is to increase the length of each line by $\frac{1}{3}$ of itself. Thus the sequence of perimeters is

$$3, \quad 3 \times (\tfrac{4}{3}), \quad 3 \times (\tfrac{4}{3})^2, \quad 3 \times (\tfrac{4}{3})^3, \ldots, \quad 3 \times (\tfrac{4}{3})^{n-1}, \ldots$$

and this increases beyond all bounds.

10.4. Further Simple Convergent Sequences of Numbers

The advent of cheap electronic calculators makes possible an investigation of convergent sequences in a way which was previously not possible.

(i) Suppose we wish to find $\sqrt{6}$ by successive approximation or by trial and error.

We know that

$$2 < \sqrt{6} < 3.$$

By squaring 2·4 and 2·5 we find that

$$2 \cdot 4 < \sqrt{6} < 2 \cdot 5.$$

The next step is

$$2\cdot44 < \sqrt{6} < 2\cdot45$$

and the next is

$$2\cdot449 < \sqrt{6} < 2\cdot450.$$

Pupils find it easy to believe that they can get as close as they please to $\sqrt{6}$ by going on long enough, although they do not know and cannot find the exact value of $\sqrt{6}$.

(ii) The classical Newton method for square root converges much more rapidly than that discussed above. It uses the idea that if x is an approximation to $\sqrt{N}$, then

$$\frac{1}{2}\left(x + \frac{N}{x}\right)$$

which is the average of x and N/x, will be a better approximation. Unlike the previous method, Newton's method improves more than one decimal place at each step. In fact it roughly doubles the number of decimal places which are correct at each step, and so is a very rewarding exercise, even if a poor first approximation is taken. For example, for $N = 2$, using 1 as a first approximation, successive approximations are

$$1, \quad 1\cdot5, \quad 1\cdot42, \quad 1\cdot4142, \quad 1\cdot414213562$$

and although the calculator then shows no further change, pupils should realize that $(1\cdot414213562)^2$ is not exactly equal to 2.

With $N = 100$ and 1 as the first approximation, the figures shown by the calculator are

$$1, \quad 50\cdot5, \quad 26\cdot2, \quad 15\cdot0, \quad 10\cdot84, \quad 10\cdot03, \quad 10\cdot0000529, \quad 10$$

This illustrates an interesting and sometimes irritating feature of some calculators; when all the figures in the range of the machine after the decimal point are zero, the calculator suppresses them. This has happened when the result given is 10.

Teachers should be aware that pupils may think that the calculator has fixed on 10 as the exact value but this is not so. A calculator which displays ten digits may store three more digits in the calculator and the number displayed will be a thirteen-digit number corrected to ten significant figures. When this corrected version is $10\cdot00000000$, the calculator simply shows 10.

10.5. Sequences given by Recurrence Relations

When a young child is asked how to get the next term of the sequence

$$2, \quad 5, \quad 10, \quad 17, \quad 26, \quad 37, \dots$$

he is much more likely to say

"you add 3, then 5, then 7, then 9, ..."

than he is to say

"it is the next perfect square, plus 1".

He prefers the *recurrence relation*, which tells how to calculate the next term of the sequence from the previous ones, to the formula for the nth term. In official mathematical language, he prefers the additive approach of the recurrence relation

$$x_1 = 2, \quad x_{n+1} = x_n + (2n + 1)$$

to the formula for the nth term,

$$x_n = n^2 + 1.$$

The formula is algebraically convenient, but makes a fresh start to the calculation of each term. For numerical calculations, a recurrence relation is often very useful. Electronic calculators make it possible for teachers to build on pupils' intuitive grasp of recurrence relations.

Several examples for use with calculators for pupils of different ages and abilities are given below. Official mathematical language is used; this language will need to be adapted according to classroom circumstances. For example, the Newton method for square root can be described by saying

"you take the average of the approximations

x and $\dfrac{N}{x}$ to get the next approximation"

rather than

$$x_{n+1} = \tfrac{1}{2}\left(x_n + \frac{N}{x_n}\right).$$

(i) If a reciprocal key is available on the calculator, the routine

$$x_{n+1} = 1 + \frac{N-1}{1+x_n}$$

is easy to use for $\sqrt{N}$.

This method does not need any intermediate writing down, but it does not converge so quickly as Newton's method. Pupils will easily see that the method does converge, but may doubt whether it converges to $\sqrt{N}$. If, for example, they take $N = 10$, and start with $x_1 = 3$, they obtain successively (to 4 decimal places)

$$3, \quad 3\cdot25, \quad 3\cdot1176, \quad 3\cdot1857, \quad 3\cdot1502, \quad 3\cdot1686, \ldots$$

so that successive values oscillate and become nearer together, sandwiching a number which lies between 3·1502 and 3·1686. An algebraic calculation then gives, if the (assumed) limit is denoted by x,

$$x = 1 + \frac{N-1}{1+x}$$

$$\Leftrightarrow x(1+x) = 1 + x + N - 1$$

$$\Leftrightarrow \quad x + x^2 = x + N$$

$$\Leftrightarrow \qquad x^2 = N$$

$$\Leftrightarrow \qquad x = \sqrt{N}, \text{ since } x \text{ is positive.}$$

(ii) If a calculator with a square root is available, a very attractive method for $N^{1/3}$ is

$$x_{n+1} = \sqrt{(\sqrt{(Nx_n)})}$$

This is extremely quick and easy, giving for $N = 10$ and $x_1 = 2$, the sequence

$$2, \quad 2\cdot1147, \quad 2\cdot1444, \quad 2\cdot1519, \quad 2\cdot1538,\ldots.$$

Again, if the (assumed) limit is x, $(x \neq 0)$,

$$x = \sqrt{(\sqrt{(Nx)})}$$
$$\Rightarrow x^4 = Nx$$
$$\Rightarrow x^3 = N.$$

(iii) By a natural method this can be extended to other integral roots. For example

$$x_{n+1} = \sqrt{\left(\sqrt{\frac{N}{x_n}}\right)} \quad \text{and} \quad x_{n+1} = \sqrt{(\sqrt{(\sqrt{(Nx_n^3)})})}$$

$$\text{and} \quad x_{n+1} = \sqrt{(\sqrt{(x_n\sqrt{(Nx_n)})})}$$

all give sequences of approximations to $N^{1/5}$.

(iv) An interesting method of finding the reciprocal of N without using division is the relation

$$x_{n+1} = 2x_n - Nx_n^2$$

Pupils might be given this relation and asked to explore what it does, for different values of N, and for different starting values. This sequence only converges to $1/N$ from starting values fairly near $1/N$, and serves as a useful antidote for pupils who are beginning to think that all sequences converge.

(v) The linear recurrence relation

$$x_{n+1} = \frac{ax_n + b}{c}$$

is well worth exploring for various values of a, b and c.

An interesting exercise is to find the temperature which is the same in $°C$ as in $°F$. This is given by $x = \frac{5}{9}(x - 32)$ and can be solved iteratively using the recurrence relation

$$x_{n+1} = \tfrac{5}{9}(x_n - 32).$$

Conversely, the temperature which is the same as $°F$ in $°C$, has the recurrence relation

$$x_{n+1} = \tfrac{9}{5}x_n + 32.$$

These two recurrence relations have different convergence properties.

(vi) Another interesting recurrence relation is

$$S_1 = a, \quad S_{n+1} = rS_n + a, \quad \text{where} \quad r < 1.$$

This gives the sum to $(n+1)$ terms of the geometric series

$$a + ar + \ldots + ar^n$$

and can be used for series such as

$$1 + \frac{1}{2} + \frac{1}{4} + \ldots + \frac{1}{2^n}$$

(vii) The following method of obtaining a sequence of rational number approximations to $\sqrt{N}$ gives the approximations in "fractional" form.

Suppose p_n and q_n are positive integers such that p_n/q_n is an approximation to $\sqrt{N}$. Then let $p_{n+1} = p_n + Nq_n$ and $q_{n+1} = p_n + q_n$.

For pupils who are familiar with matrix notation it may be convenient to use the notation

$$\begin{pmatrix} p_{n+1} \\ q_{n+1} \end{pmatrix} = \begin{pmatrix} 1 & N \\ 1 & 1 \end{pmatrix} \begin{pmatrix} p_n \\ q_n \end{pmatrix}.$$

Then p_{n+1}/q_{n+1} is a better approximation to $\sqrt{N}$ than p_n/q_n.

We give an example for $N = 3$ taking $p_1 = q_1 = 1$. The calculator is used only to verify how the sequence is converging. Successive terms are

$$\frac{1}{1}, \ \frac{4}{2}, \ \frac{10}{6}, \ \frac{28}{16}, \ \frac{76}{44}, \ \frac{208}{120}, \ \frac{568}{328}, \ \frac{1552}{896}, \ldots$$

We note that $(\frac{1552}{896})^2 = 3{\cdot}0003\ldots$ The reader should consider why this method works.

(viii) In two articles in *Mathematics Teaching**, Dr. T. J. Fletcher shows an ingenious and effective method of approximating using vectors. The article would give excellent material for workcards, and once again shows sandwich methods at work.

(ix) The calculator is particularly useful for solving equations of the type $x = f(x)$ by using the recurrence relation $x_{n+1} = f(x_n)$ with a suitable starting point. This does not always work, as some of the above examples illustrate, but it works often enough to be worth trying. A good elementary discussion, though not suitable for pupils before the sixth form, is found in *Elementary Calculus and Co-ordinate Geometry II* by C. G. Nobbs, OUP, p. 339.

(x) The matrix

$$\begin{pmatrix} 0{\cdot}5 & 0{\cdot}2 \\ 0{\cdot}5 & 0{\cdot}8 \end{pmatrix}$$

maps the vectors

$$\begin{pmatrix} 1 \\ 0 \end{pmatrix} \quad \text{and} \quad \begin{pmatrix} 0 \\ 1 \end{pmatrix} \quad \text{to} \quad \begin{pmatrix} 0{\cdot}5 \\ 0{\cdot}5 \end{pmatrix} \quad \text{and} \quad \begin{pmatrix} 0{\cdot}2 \\ 0{\cdot}8 \end{pmatrix}$$

respectively. Then the matrix maps

$$\begin{pmatrix} 0.5 \\ 0.5 \end{pmatrix} \quad \text{and} \quad \begin{pmatrix} 0.2 \\ 0.8 \end{pmatrix}$$

to

$$\begin{pmatrix} 0.5 & 0.2 \\ 0.5 & 0.8 \end{pmatrix}\begin{pmatrix} 0.5 \\ 0.5 \end{pmatrix} = \begin{pmatrix} 0.35 \\ 0.65 \end{pmatrix} \quad \text{and} \quad \begin{pmatrix} 0.5 & 0.2 \\ 0.5 & 0.8 \end{pmatrix}\begin{pmatrix} 0.2 \\ 0.8 \end{pmatrix} = \begin{pmatrix} 0.26 \\ 0.74 \end{pmatrix}.$$

Writing

$$\begin{pmatrix} 1 \\ 0 \end{pmatrix} \quad \text{and} \quad \begin{pmatrix} 0 \\ 1 \end{pmatrix}$$

as OP_1 and OQ_1 respectively, their images as OP_2 and OQ_2, and so on, this situation is illustrated by figure 10.9. What happens subsequently?

10.6. Some Mathematical Discussion

We return to the geometrical example in section 10.3 of a sequence of squares and rectangles.

The following conversation was heard between two pupils aged 14 of average ability in a classroom in the North of England:

> *Angela*: You're wasting your time. You'll never fill that corner in.
> *Gary*: I could if my pencil was sharper.
> *Angela*: No, you couldn't.
> *Gary*: I could draw more squares than you.
> *Angela*: You still couldn't fill the corner in.

Angela and Gary's conversation shows a clear intuitive grasp of

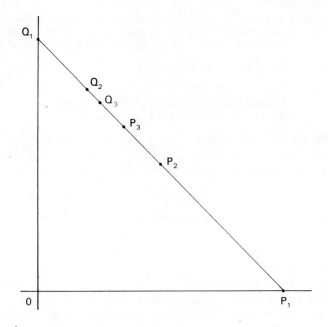

Figure 10.9

some important points about a sequence which converges to a limit. These are:

(i) "You'll never fill that corner in". Angela realizes that it is impossible to do more than a finite sequence of operations. At the nth step of the construction, n may be very large, but it is always *finite*. We can never take an infinite number of steps.

(ii) In Gary's mind, the distinction between a particular term of the sequence and the *limit* of the sequence is not clear. He realizes that by taking enough steps, he can get as close as he pleases to an area of $2\,dm^2$. However, he seems to think that, if he drew enough squares and rectangles, he would actually reach $2\,dm^2$. In fact, if A_n is the area after n steps, we have (see figure 10.3)

$$A_n < 2 \quad \text{for every whole number } n.$$

(iii) Gary is clear, however, in his assertion of superiority "I can draw more squares than you", that however many terms of the sequence Angela has drawn, more terms are always possible, and that the area always increases.

Between them they realize that

$$A_1 < A_2 < A_3 < \ldots < A_n < A_{n+1} < \ldots < 2$$

and that the difference between A_n and 2 can be made as small as we please by taking n large enough.

In the class discussion which followed this experiment, the pupils were equally divided between two points of view. The area had now been represented arithmetically on the blackboard as

$$1 + \tfrac{1}{2} + \tfrac{1}{4} + \tfrac{1}{8} + \ldots$$

Some pupils thought that the sum must always be less than 2 ("'cos you can't fill the corner in."). Others maintained that eventually the sum would exceed 2 ("You keep on adding more—it must get bigger".)

In order that pupils gain the maximum of understanding about limits from this and similar examples involving summation, it is important to use a notation which hides nothing; the usual notation

$$1 + \tfrac{1}{2} + \tfrac{1}{4} + \tfrac{1}{8} + \ldots = 2$$

hides a great deal, and should not be used at this stage.

The pupils' attention should be focused on two points: clarity about successive steps of the process, and the size of the difference between each member of the sequence (A_n) of areas and 2.

	Area filled/dm²		*Area unfilled/dm²*
1st step	1		1
2nd step	$1 + \tfrac{1}{2}$	$= 1\tfrac{1}{2}$	$\tfrac{1}{2}$
3rd step	$1 + \tfrac{1}{2} + \tfrac{1}{4}$	$= 1\tfrac{3}{4}$	$\tfrac{1}{4}$
4th step	$1 + \tfrac{1}{2} + \tfrac{1}{4} + \tfrac{1}{8}$	$= 1\tfrac{7}{8}$	$\tfrac{1}{8}$
5th step	$1 + \tfrac{1}{2} + \tfrac{1}{4} + \tfrac{1}{8} + \tfrac{1}{16}$	$= 1\tfrac{15}{16}$	$\tfrac{1}{16}$
nth step	$1 + \tfrac{1}{2} + \tfrac{1}{4} + \ldots + \dfrac{1}{2^{n-1}}$		$\dfrac{1}{2^{n-1}}$

More-able pupils will be able to see that at the nth step, the number of dm² filled is

$$1 + \frac{1}{2} + \frac{1}{4} + \ldots + \frac{1}{2^{n-1}} = 2 - \frac{1}{2^{n-1}}.$$

The unfilled area of $1/2^{n-1}$ dm² can be made as small as we please by taking enough steps, but for every n there always is an unfilled area. At this stage, the following wording should be used, without mention of limits:

We can make the filled area A_n as close as we please to 2 dm² by taking a large enough number of steps. The filled area converges to 2 dm².

The pupils' attention can also be drawn to the fact that we have a sequence of numbers

$$1, \quad 1\tfrac{1}{2}, \quad 1\tfrac{3}{4}, \quad 1\tfrac{7}{8}, \quad 1\tfrac{15}{16}, \ldots,$$

in which the terms are always increasing, but all the terms remain less than 2. This sequence, which is bounded above, is of a fundamentally different nature from the many sequences already familiar to the pupils, such as

$$2, \quad 3, \quad 5, \quad 8, \quad 12, \ldots,$$

which increase beyond all bounds.

"Achilles and the tortoise" provides another situation which can usefully be linked to the last one. It also has the advantage that pupils are likely to start off not knowing exactly where or when Achilles catches the tortoise. A step-by-step analysis with a distance-time graph is helpful.

To simplify the numbers, we use a rather speedy tortoise. "Achilles can run twice as fast as the tortoise, so he gives the tortoise a kilometre start. While Achilles runs the kilometre, the tortoise runs $\tfrac{1}{2}$ km; then while Achilles runs that $\tfrac{1}{2}$ km, the tortoise runs $\tfrac{1}{4}$ km; and so on."

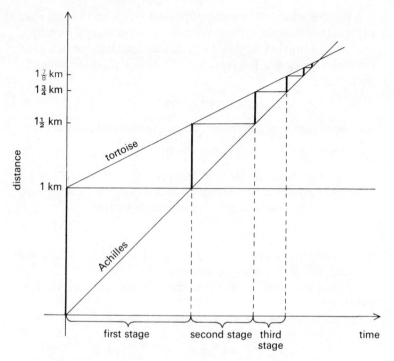

Figure 10.10   Distance-time graph for "Achilles and the tortoise".

Distances in km from Achilles' starting point

	Achilles	Tortoise
To start with	0	1
After one stage	1	$1 + \frac{1}{2}$
After two stages	$1 + \frac{1}{2}$	$1 + \frac{1}{2} + \frac{1}{4}$
After three stages	$1 + \frac{1}{2} + \frac{1}{4}$	$1 + \frac{1}{2} + \frac{1}{4} + \frac{1}{8}$

After a few stages, pupils will be certain that Achilles catches the tortoise at the 2 km mark, and should then record the distances of the two participants from this point at each stage.

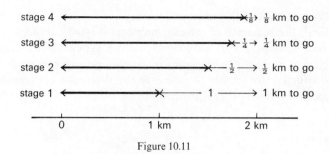

Figure 10.11

If we take another form of the problem, in which Achilles is ten times as fast as the tortoise, a decimal representation is useful:

Distances in km from Achilles' starting-point

	Achilles	Tortoise
To start with	0	1
After one stage	1	$1 + \frac{1}{10} = 1 \cdot 1$
After two stages	$1 + \frac{1}{10} = 1 \cdot 1$	$1 + \frac{1}{10} + \frac{1}{100} = 1 \cdot 11$
After three stages	$1 + \frac{1}{10} + \frac{1}{100} = 1 \cdot 11$	$1 + \frac{1}{10} + \frac{1}{100} + \frac{1}{1000} = 1 \cdot 111$

The catching-up point is not so obvious here, although pupils who are familiar with recurring decimals will realize that the sequence

$$1, \quad 1 \cdot 1, \quad 1 \cdot 11, \quad 1 \cdot 111, \ldots.$$

converges to $1\frac{1}{9}$.

This leads us to non-terminating decimals.

10.7. Non-Terminating Decimals

In the last chapter, we used sandwiching methods to discuss non-terminating decimals. For example,

$$0 \cdot 3 \quad \leqslant \tfrac{1}{3} \leqslant 0 \cdot 4$$
$$0 \cdot 33 \quad \leqslant \tfrac{1}{3} \leqslant 0 \cdot 34$$
$$0 \cdot 333 \leqslant \tfrac{1}{3} \leqslant 0 \cdot 334$$

and so on.

84

We can think of this in several ways.

First, the sequence of rational numbers 0.3, 0.33, 0.333, ..., is *increasing*, and it is also bounded above by $\frac{1}{3}$. We can, however, get as close as we please to $\frac{1}{3}$ by going on far enough in this sequence. It is instructive for pupils to calculate the difference between the successive terms of the sequence and $\frac{1}{3}$:

$$\frac{1}{3} - \frac{3}{10} = \frac{1}{30}$$
$$\frac{1}{3} - \frac{33}{100} = \frac{1}{300}$$
$$\frac{1}{3} - \frac{333}{1000} = \frac{1}{3000}$$

and so on.

We say that the sequence

$$0.3, \quad 0.33, \quad 0.333, \ldots, \quad \text{converges to } \tfrac{1}{3}.$$

Similarly, the second sequence

$$0.4, \quad 0.34, \quad 0.334, \ldots.$$

is *decreasing*, all its terms are greater than $\frac{1}{3}$, and it also converges to $\frac{1}{3}$ because the terms can be made as close as we please to $\frac{1}{3}$ by going on far enough in the sequence.

Alternatively, we may look at the successive sandwich inequalities, note that the thickness of the sandwiches can be made as

Sandwich	Thickness of sandwich
$0.3 \leqslant \frac{1}{3} \leqslant 0.4$	0.1
$0.33 \leqslant \frac{1}{3} \leqslant 0.34$	0.01
$0.333 \leqslant \frac{1}{3} \leqslant 0.334$	0.001

small as we please by going on far enough and that there is one number, $\frac{1}{3}$, which is common to all the sandwich inequalities. This is sufficient to show that both the sequences

$$0.3, \quad 0.33, \quad 0.333 \ldots$$

and

$$0.4, \quad 0.34, \quad 0.334 \ldots$$

converge to $\frac{1}{3}$.

A number which often baffles pupils is $0.999\ldots$ or $0.\dot{9}$. They may say that the difference between $0.\dot{9}$ and 1 is "point nought recurring, one", indicating that they do not yet understand the significance of the recurring figure. The sequence of rational approximations to $0.\dot{9}$ is

$$0.9, \quad 0.99, \quad 0.999, \ldots$$

and the sequence of differences between these numbers and 1 is

$$0.1, \quad 0.01, \quad 0.001, \ldots.$$

Thus we can make the rational number $0.999\ldots9$ as close as we please to 1 by going on far enough in the sequence. It is perhaps unfortunate for young pupils that this fact is written

$$0.\dot{9} = 1$$

in the same way that we write $0.\dot{3} = \frac{1}{3}$. What is meant is that the sequence $0.9, 0.99, 0.999, \ldots$ converges to 1.

Appropriate forms of words to discuss these phenomena with pupils are:

(i) $0.\dot{3}$ is the number whose approximations are

$$0.3, \quad 0.33, \quad 0.333, \ldots.$$

The approximation can be made as close as we please to $\frac{1}{3}$, so we say

$$0.\dot{3} = \tfrac{1}{3}.$$

(ii) $0.\dot{9}$ is the number whose approximations are

$$0.9, \quad 0.99, \quad 0.999, \ldots.$$

The approximation can be made as close as we please to 1, so we say

$$0.\dot{9} = 1.$$

10.8. The Key Idea

Suppose we have a sequence of numbers. We shall say that this sequence *converges to a number* or *approaches a limit* if we can convince ourselves that we can get as close as we please to this number or limit by going on far enough in the sequence.

We shall use this key idea

> We can get as close as we please to…

again and again, for it is the essential first step in developing the limit concept.

What we cannot do, and it would not be appropriate to try in any systematic way with sixteen-year-old pupils, is to prove in all the examples we have given that the sequences have limits. At this age, an intuitive grasp of the idea of a limit should be the objective.

10.9. A Sandwich Inequality Argument for Convergence

The search for $\sqrt{6}$ discussed in section 10.4 provides an interesting example of a sequence for which the convergence can be proved by using a sandwich inequality.

In this work we established that

$$2\cdot4 \ < \sqrt{6} < 2\cdot5$$
$$2\cdot44 < \sqrt{6} < 2\cdot45$$

and so on.

It is not possible here to find how close $2\cdot4$, $2\cdot44$, etc., are to $\sqrt{6}$. However, we can guarantee that at each stage the differences between the upper and lower approximations get smaller, and can be made as close to zero as we please, by going on far enough in the sequence. The differences between $\sqrt{6}$ and the rational number

approximations to $\sqrt{6}$ must also decrease, so an approximation can be found which is as close as we please to $\sqrt{6}$.

Lower approximation	*Upper approximation*	*Difference between $\sqrt{6}$ and each approximation*
2	3	Less than 1
2·4	2·5	Less than 0·1
2·44	2·45	Less than 0·01
2·449	2·450	Less than 0·001

Hence we say that the sequence of rational approximations 2, 2·4, 2·44, 2·449, … converges to $\sqrt{6}$.

10.10. Fibonacci Sequences

Sometimes the sandwich argument needs to be used rather differently. Fibonacci sequences provide an example.

The standard Fibonacci sequence has 0, 1 as its first two terms. Each successive term is then the sum of the two previous terms, so that the sequence is

$$0, \quad 1, \quad 1, \quad 2, \quad 3, \quad 5, \quad 8, \quad 13, \quad 21, \quad 34, \dots.$$

This is, however, only the simplest example of a whole class of Fibonacci sequences, as a Fibonacci sequence can be constructed for any choice of first two terms.

The ratios of successive terms of a Fibonacci sequence can be calculated to give a new sequence. The standard sequence has as its sequence of ratios

$$1, \quad 2, \quad 1\cdot5, \quad 1\cdot6, \quad 1\cdot6, \quad 1.625, \quad 1\cdot615384, \quad 1\cdot619047\dots$$

This sequence has two interesting properties.

(i) It does its own sandwiching, successive terms being alternately greater and less than the preceding term. In fact, we can split the sequence into two sequences, one of which is increasing and the other decreasing:

$$1, \quad 1{\cdot}5, \quad 1{\cdot}6, \quad 1{\cdot}615384,\ldots$$
$$2, \quad 1{\cdot}6, \quad 1{\cdot}625, \quad 1{\cdot}619047,\ldots$$

(ii) It can be seen that if this pattern continues, and if the terms of the upper sequence can be made as close as we please to those of the lower sequence, there will be a number sandwiched in between them. It is intuitively clear that the sequence of ratios converges to a number whose value is $1{\cdot}61\ldots$, although we cannot say precisely what number this is. In the case of this sequence, we are sure that it converges, although we cannot write down an expression for its limit. This is in contrast to the example of section 10.9, when we knew the limit was $\sqrt{6}$.

10.11. Conclusion

In each activity in this chapter, pupils will have the specific objective of investigating a particular situation, but the teacher will also have in mind the growth of the concept of a limit. It is helpful if he uses forms of words such as "Can you get as close as you please to the number? (or the curve, or the point?)"

The limits discussed in this chapter are largely limits "at infinity", although we have not used the phrase. They form a very useful preparation for the limits "at a point" used in differentiation, and this preliminary work is important not only in enabling pupils to tackle differentiation with understanding, but also in keeping mathematics alive as an investigating exploratory subject in the years preceding the $16+$ examinations. Nearly all this work can and should be done in play-like activities in which the limit idea can develop over several years before being applied in the context of differentiation. The key concept in all work on limits is that *we can get as close as we please by* . . . In different settings, we get "as close as we please" in different ways. The first two examples are drawn from this chapter, while the third and fourth look forward to chapter 12.

(i) We get as close as we please to the limit of a sequence *by going far enough in the sequence.*

(ii) We get as close as we please in drawing a curve of pursuit *by taking short enough steps.*

(iii) We get as close as we please to the tangent to a curve at P *by taking a chord through points P and Q which are close enough together.*

(iv) We get as close as we please to the actual velocity of a particle *by taking the average velocity over a short enough interval.*

Formal work on differentiation and other limit ideas at the next stage will be much more intelligible to pupils if the limit idea is allowed to grow slowly and informally before the official notation for limits is introduced.

11 Area under a Graph: Velocity and Displacement

11.1. Introduction

The idea that area under a graph can convey useful information should not be new to pupils, because it can be brought out in graphical work in the late primary school or early secondary school in the context of block graphs or histograms. More could be made of this aspect of area in the early years in the secondary school. For instance, in the block graph in figure 11.1 the shaded area under the graph tells us the total number of pupils in the class.

If a new pupil were to arrive, and information about him were added to the graph, the height of one of the columns would be increased by one unit and hence an additional area of one unit square would be shaded. Areas of histograms will become more significant and important in later studies of statistics, but an early introduction to the interpretation of areas under graphs would be most profitable.

In this chapter we concentrate on velocity-time graphs and on the problem of convincing pupils that the area under a velocity-time graph gives a measure of displacement. Many traditional books and courses do not include this work, but a number of modern courses for average and more-able pupils do.

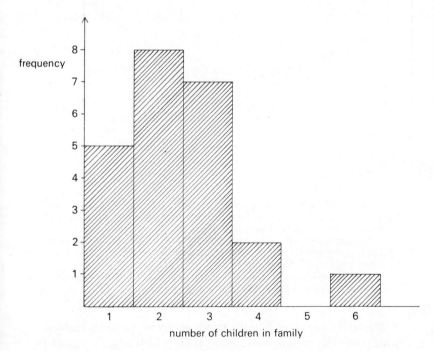

Figure 11.1   Block graph of the number of children in each family for a class.

11.2. The SMP Treatment of Area under the Velocity-Time Graph

The treatment of area under a velocity-time graph in *SMP Book X*, p. 174, is quoted below.

3   Areas under graphs

(a) A lorry carrying a wide, heavy load travels at a speed of 10 km/h for 3 hours and at 7 km/h for the next 2 hours. How far has the lorry travelled?

(b) A speed-time graph for the lorry's journey is shown in Figure 13.

How many of the red squares can be fitted into the shaded area? We can see that the area of the red square represents a distance of 1 km. Hence the total area under the graph represents a distance of 44 km, i.e. the area under the graph represents the total distance travelled by the lorry. [Red is shown here shaded.]

(c) Figure 14 shows a speed-time graph for a car travelling along a motorway

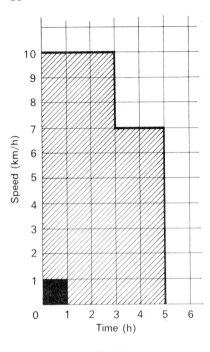

Fig. 13.

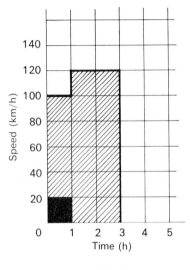

Fig. 14.

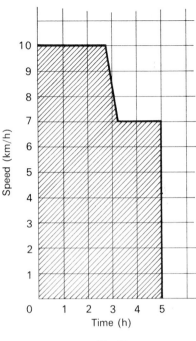

Fig. 15.

at a constant speed of 100 km/h for 1 hour and then at a constant speed of 120 km/h for 2 hours.

Do you agree that the red square represents a distance of 20 km? How many of the red squares can be fitted into the shaded area? What is the total distance travelled by the car?

(d) The graphs in sections (b) and (c) represent idealized situations. Lorries and cars cannot, in fact, change speeds instantaneously as the graphs suggest. A more realistic description of the lorry's journey is represented by Figure 15.

Use the graph to describe the lorry's journey in words. Calculate the area under the graph and hence write down the distance the lorry travelled.

Now sketch a more realistic version of the car's journey than that represented by Figure 14. Do not forget that the car has to travel a total distance of 340 km.

(e) The rate at which industrial waste flows into a river from a factory increases during the first two hours of a working day until it reaches a maximum. The waste is then produced at this constant rate for 4 hours. After this it decreases. The graph in Figure 16 shows the amount of waste per hour flowing into the river at various times during the day.

The shaded rectangle represents a quantity of 5000 litres of industrial waste. The area of triangle A is $\frac{1}{2} \times 2 \times 15 = 15$. Thus the area of region A represents a quantity of 15 000 litres of waste.

Calculate (i) the area of region B; (ii) the area of region C. Hence write down the total amount of waste flowing from the factory per day.

The technique of leading the pupils gently into a new situation, which is so ably used in this exercise, is one which is familiar to and used by all teachers. The pupils are first convinced that the area

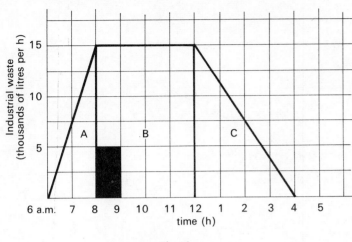

Fig. 16.

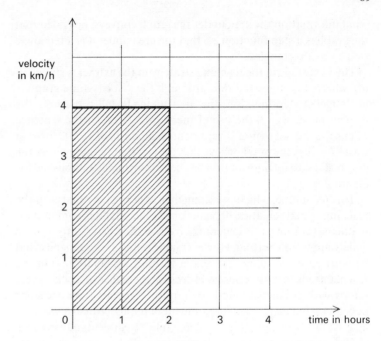

Figure 11.2

under a velocity-time graph represents the displacement in the simple case in which *the velocity-time graph is a step-function*. Care needs to be taken over this stage, for pupils are accustomed to representing displacement by a *length* on a graph, and it is a further abstraction to use a number of units of area to represent a number of units of displacement. Fortunately, it is easy for the pupil to relate

$$displacement = velocity \times time$$

to the area of a rectangle whose length represents velocity and whose breadth represents time. The units are a great help, and for instance in figure 11.2, the shaded area represents a displacement of 8 km, and is a quantity whose units are

$$\frac{kilometres}{hours} \times hours$$

or kilometres.

Similarly, in the industrial waste example in the extract, one axis represents litres per hour, and the other represents hours, so the area represents

$$\frac{litres}{hours} \times hours,$$

or litres. This is a very effective way of remembering or working out what information the area under the graph conveys, provided that the graph is a step-function, so that the area under it is a rectangle or a sum of rectangles.

The next stage in the teaching strategy in the extract is shown in (*d*), where it is suggested that although the velocity-time graph is no longer a step-function, the area under it still represents the displacement. By (*e*) the use of the word "Thus" in the sentence "Thus the area of region *A* represents a quantity of 15 000 litres of waste." makes the pupil believe that the fact that the area under the graph gives useful information has been thoroughly established for all graphs.

This technique, which is extremely useful in many places in the teaching of mathematics, depends on the fact that it is common for mathematical ideas to generalize from simple cases into a more widely applicable setting. However, able pupils may recognize and be worried when jumps are made without explanation, and the teacher needs to make conscious decisions whether to discuss these jumps with particular pupils or groups of pupils. The decisions depend on balancing the development of pupils' critical awareness against the degree of difficulty that a fuller treatment may involve.

Unfortunately, when an attempt is made to justify the representation of displacement by area under a velocity-time graph, a fallacious argument is sometimes used, and this is described in section 11.3.

There is available, however, a straightforward argument which forms an important step towards the understanding of integration, and which is intelligible and convincing to pupils. This argument is discussed in section 11.4.

11.3. An Incorrect Argument

Consider a particle which accelerates uniformly from a velocity of 2 m/s to a velocity of 4 m/s in 2 seconds. Its velocity-time graph is

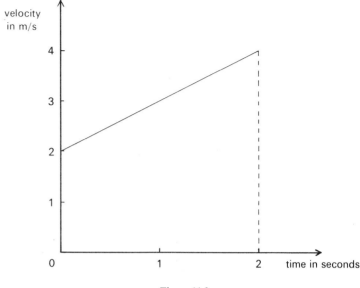

Figure 11.3

shown in figure 11.3. The argument runs as follows. As the particle starts with velocity 2 m/s and finishes with velocity 4 m/s, the average of its initial and final velocities is 3 m/s. Thus it might be regarded as travelling for 2 seconds at an average velocity of 3 m/s, so that it covers a distance of 6 metres. Also, the number of units of area below the graph is

$$\frac{2+4}{2} \times 2 = 6.$$

Hence this example might be thought to illustrate the result that the area under a velocity-time graph represents the displacement, even when the velocity is not constant.

However, *in general*, the average of the initial and final velocities is not equal to the average velocity. It will be recalled that

$$\text{average velocity} = \frac{\text{total displacement}}{\text{time taken}}.$$

This is not in general equal to

$$\tfrac{1}{2}(\text{initial velocity} + \text{final velocity}).$$

The fallacy can be seen clearly by considering a particle which travels at 2 m/s for 49 s, and then at 12 m/s for 1 s. In this time it has a displacement of $(98 + 12)$ m $= 110$ m, and so has an average velocity of $\frac{110}{50}$ m/s, or 2·2 m/s, but the average of its initial and final velocities is $\tfrac{1}{2}(2 + 12)$ m/s or 7 m/s.

It is only when a particle moves with *constant acceleration* that its average velocity is equal to the average of its initial and final velocities. In this case the velocity-time graph is a trapezium, whose area is found by multiplying the average of its two parallel sides by its width. To establish correctly in the previous example that the average velocity is 3 m/s, it is necessary first to calculate that the displacement in the 2 seconds of the journey is 6 metres.

11.4. A Sandwiching Argument for Displacement and Area

A straightforward and convincing sandwiching argument can be used to demonstrate that the area under a velocity-time graph still represents the displacement, even when the velocity is not constant.

It is clear that the fact that, for constant velocity, the area under a velocity-time graph represents the displacement, extends immediately to the situation where the velocity-time graph is a step-function (figure 11.4). The extension to other velocity-time graphs can then be developed as follows.

A man X walks with a variable velocity illustrated in the velocity-time graph of figure 11.5(i).

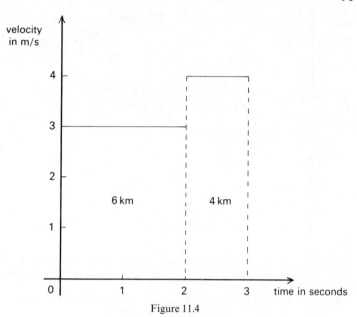

Figure 11.4

We now put alongside X a slow man S and a fast man F who walk with the constant velocities shown in figure 11.5(ii).

Two inequalities can now be written down from the pupils' intuitive insight. First, it is clear to them that between the times $t = 1$ and $t = 9$

area under graph of S $\leqslant$ area under graph of X $\leqslant$ area under graph of F.

Secondly, they know that

the faster you go, the further you get in the time

so because S is always walking slower than X, and F is always walking faster than X,

displacement of S $\leqslant$ displacement of X $\leqslant$ displacement of F.

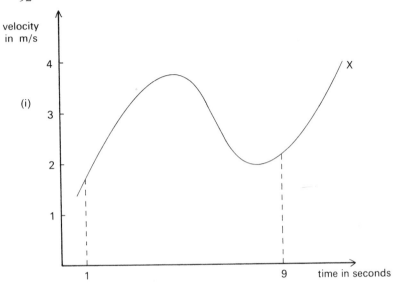

(i)

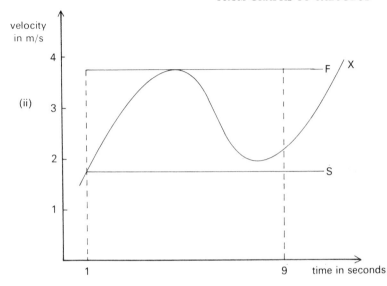

(ii)

Figure 11.5   A sandwiching representation connecting displacement with the area
under a velocity-time graph.

Clearly a sandwich argument is going to develop.

It has already been established that, for step-function velocity-time graphs such as those of S and F, the displacement is represented by the area under the velocity-time graph. Thus the two sets of inequalities can be put together

area under graph of S	⩽ area under graph of X ⩽	area under graph of F
represents		*represents*
displacement of S	⩽ displacement of X ⩽	displacement of F

The two quantities in each box are equal in magnitude, but it is important to realize that the pupils have yet to be convinced that the area under the graph of X represents the displacement of X. Now for most of the time S is walking considerably slower than X.

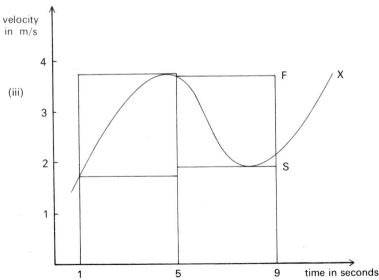

(iii)

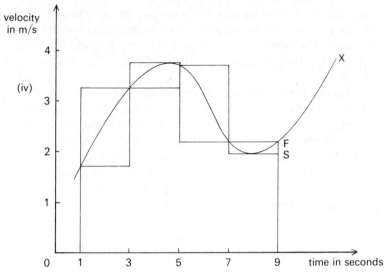

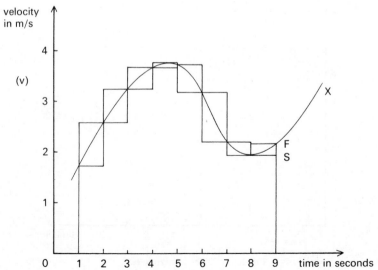

He could be allowed to speed up for some of the time and still always be walking slower than X. Hence at half-time (or some other convenient time) his velocity is instantaneously adjusted as shown in figure 11.5(iii). The velocity of F is similarly adjusted.

The same two inequalities still hold:

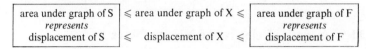

Now another two instantaneous changes of the velocities of S and F are put in, as shown in figure 11.5(iv).

It is still true that

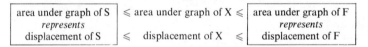

More instantaneous changes of velocity for S and F can be introduced (figure 11.5(v)), and it still remains true that

area under graph of S	$\leqslant$ area under graph of X $\leqslant$	area under graph of F
represents		*represents*
displacement of S	$\leqslant$ displacement of X $\leqslant$	displacement of F

At this stage pupils should be convinced that the inequalities hold, however many times the velocities of S and F are adjusted. The areas under the graphs of S and F get closer together, and the displacements of S and F also get closer together. Moreover, and this is the crucial point, the displacements of S and F can be made *as close together as we please* by the same process.

It follows from the sandwiching assumption of section 9.7, and it will seem evident to pupils, that only one number is sandwiched between the areas of all possible graphs S and the areas of all possible graphs F. This number is the area under the graph of X, and represents the displacement of X.

It should be made clear by examples that these ideas do not only apply to velocity-time graphs, but also to other graphs such as that given as example (*e*) in the *SMP* extract. The reason that velocity-time graphs are dealt with first is that pupils are more familiar with velocity than they are with other rates.

11.5. Negative Velocity and Negative Area

A distinction needs to be made between the use of the word *area* in chapter 7, and some implications of its use in this chapter. The *area of a plane* figure, discussed in chapter 7, is always regarded as positive, whereas the *area under the graph of a function* needs to be

regarded as positive or negative according as the values of the function are positive or negative. The reason for this is shown by the following example. The parallel between displacement and area having been established, it needs to be maintained in all situations.

Consider the velocity-time graph of the particle X shown in figure 11.6. Between the times $t = 2$ and $t = 4$, X is travelling with a positive but decreasing velocity. At 4 seconds it instantaneously stops and starts off again in the opposite direction. Hence at the end of 10 seconds it has travelled a distance represented by the area A in figure 11.6 forwards, and a distance represented by the area B backwards. In order that the total area under the graph should represent the *displacement* at the end of the journey, area B must

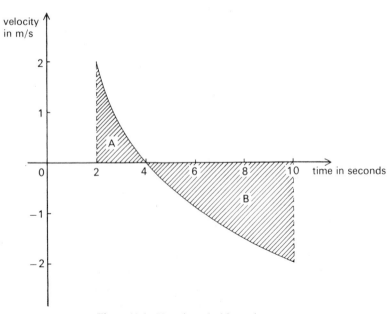

Figure 11.6   Negative velocities and areas.

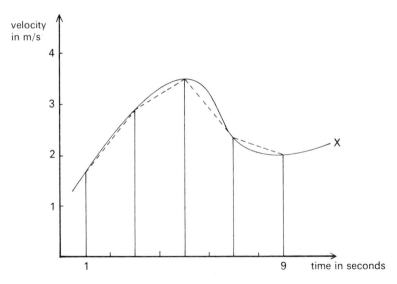

Figure 11.7   The trapezium rule.

be regarded as negative. Pupils should be aware that it is not an arbitrary decision that areas below the x-axis are regarded as negative.

11.6. The Trapezium Rule

In numerical work, pupils will often obtain sandwich inequalities for the area under a graph, as suggested above. If an approximate numerical value is needed for an area under a graph, instead of a pair of inequalities, the trapezium rule is the best method for pupils at this level to use.

It is not clear in speech whether the trapezium rule refers to the *idea* of dividing the region under the graph into trapezia and then saying that the area under the graph is approximately equal to the sum of the areas of the trapezia, or whether the trapezium rule refers to the *formula* to which the idea leads.

The idea is much more important than the formula. Formulae are never easy to remember, and the trapezium-rule formula is no exception. In more advanced work other formulae are nearly always used when approximating to areas under graphs, and in elementary work it always suffices to calculate the area of each trapezium in turn. The calculation of areas under graphs is discussed further in chapter 13.

12 Velocity and Gradient

12.1. The Tangent to a Curve

This chapter is concerned with the idea of a tangent to a graph and with developing the relationship between the gradient of a tangent and velocity. This is generalized so that other rates of change are also linked with gradients.

A number of diverse ideas from various realms of experience need to have come together if pupils are to understand the idea of a tangent to a curve.

Curve stitching (figure 10.4) shows how a line can make a very close approximation to a curve at a particular point. Each stitch forms a tangent to the curve, and the curve is enveloped by all the tangents.

The actual direction of motion of a point travelling along a curve is also an important part of the tangent concept. Young pupils often have an actively wrong idea about this. They think that when the string of a conker breaks, the conker flies out along the direction of the string; they think that when two children whirl one another around and lose their grasp, they will fall directly outwards. This idea needs to be replaced by the explicit idea that the direction of motion in a curved path is along the tangent.

Examples from athletics are helpful here, and can often be clearly seen on television in slow motion. When a discus or hammer is released it starts to move in the direction along the curve which the thrower described with it, that is, along the tangent to the curve. A runner rounding a bend is at any instant running in the direction of the tangent to the bend. A fielder catching a cricket ball recoils in the direction of the tangent to the ball's path.

Discussion of such examples as these will help pupils to become explicitly aware that the tangent to a curve at a point is the straight

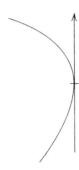

Figure 12.1

line which shows the direction of the curve at that point. The tangent may also be considered as the straight line which fits the curve most closely in the neighbourhood of that point (figure 12.1).

Later in the chapter it will be seen how much information is conveyed by the *gradient* of a curve. So far gradients have only been mentioned in the context of straight lines, so it is natural to try to define the gradient of a curve at a point as the gradient of the tangent line to the curve at that point. This is why, before any of the subsequent work in this chapter is attempted, it is important for pupils to have well-developed intuitive ideas about tangents to curves.

These points are well brought out in the following extract taken from *Modern Mathematics for Schools*, Book 7, p. 42.

---

2 *The gradient of a curve*

Figure 5 shows an aircraft coming in to land. The direction of travel of the aircraft at a point P on the flight path is the same as the direction of the tangent

at P. The gradient of the tangent at P gives a measure of the steepness of the curve at P.

The gradient of a curve changes from point to point, and the gradient of the curve at P is defined to be the *gradient of the tangent to the curve* at P.

12.2. The Need for the Gradient of a Curve

In chapter 8, straight-line graphs were used as models of the way in which the displacement of an object moving at constant velocity depends on the time taken. In the real world, cars, trains, runners and swimmers do not move with constant velocity. In these cases the straight line may not be a good model, and pupils may recognize this. The question which then arises is how to calculate velocity at an instant from a curved displacement-time graph in the same way that the speedometer of a car indicates the velocity of the car at an instant.

Pupils should first recognize from a number of numerical examples that if a graph is drawn showing the position of a runner at each instant, then his average velocity over any period of time corresponds to the gradient of a chord of the graph.

Referring to figure 12.2, the average velocity between the times a

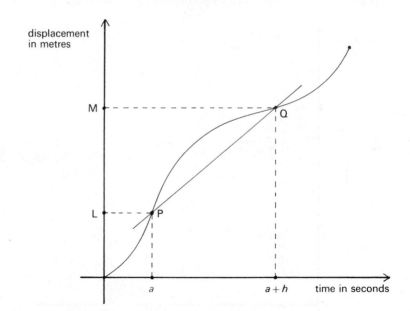

Figure 12.2

and $a+h$ is found by dividing the displacement LM by the time interval h. This average velocity must be recognized and identified as the gradient of the chord PQ.

If pupils feel, in figure 12.2, that at P the runner is actually going faster than the average velocity calculated, then they are beginning to see that the gradient of the curve itself will correspond to the actual velocity at P.

The way forward to establishing the link between actual velocity and gradient of a curve more firmly is to shorten the time interval over which the average velocity is calculated. In figure 12.3, average velocities over the time intervals h_1, h_2 and h_3 correspond to the gradients of the chords PQ_1, PQ_2 and PQ_3 respectively. On any graph which a pupil draws, the chords PQ for which Q is very

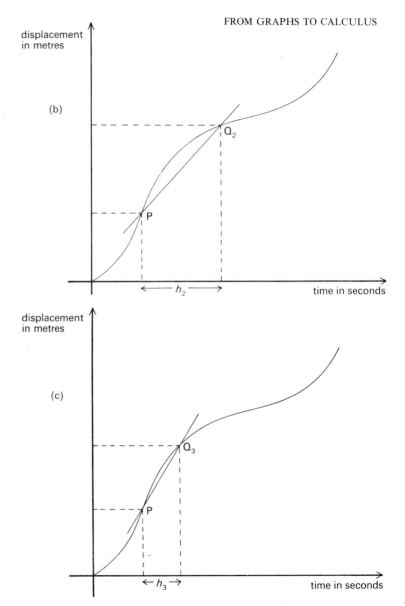

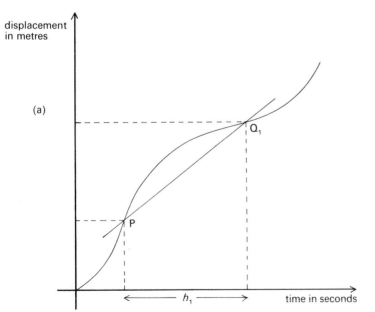

Figure 12.3 Approximations to instantaneous velocity through the link with the gradient of a displacement-time curve.

close to P are very difficult to distinguish from the curve itself in the neighbourhood of P. This leads easily to the conviction that the "actual velocity" at P is given by the gradient of the tangent to the curve drawn at P.

It is true that mathematical difficulties can arise in trying to be precise in explaining what is meant by "velocity at an instant" or "gradient of a curve", and mathematical purists may say that neither concept is yet properly defined. At this stage this is unimportant, for the concepts of "velocity at an instant" and "gradient of a curve" are intuitively clear to pupils. It is much more important for these concepts to be linked in the minds of the pupils than it is for pupils to be able to articulate clearly and concisely what the concepts mean. In fact, the concepts of velocity and gradient are strengthened by the link between them, and precise definitions are inappropriate until after that link has been made.

12.3. Gradients of Tangents by Drawing

It is now that pupils can usefully do examples in which they calculate velocity at a point by drawing a tangent to a displacement-time graph using a ruler and pencil, and by calculating the gradient of their tangent line from measurements made from their graph. They can also learn through examples that the gradient of a curve is useful in other circumstances.

For instance, a domestic gas meter measures the volume of gas used by the householder, and it is possible to draw a graph of the volume of gas used against time. This might have the general characteristics of figure 12.4.

In this example, the gradients of chords and tangents give information about the average rate of flow of gas and the actual rate of flow of gas. The gradient of the tangent at P corresponds to the *rate of change of the volume of gas* at P.

Another example in which gradient is useful is provided by acceleration. In the same way that the average velocity of a moving body is calculated by measuring changes of displacement in a given time, so also its acceleration can be calculated by measuring

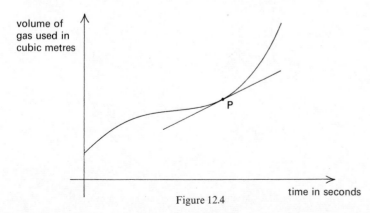

Figure 12.4

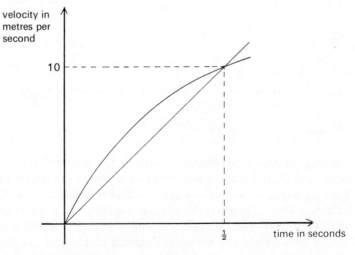

Figure 12.5

changes of velocity in a given time. A sprinter who starts from rest and reaches a velocity of 10 metres per second in half a second has an average acceleration over that time of 20 metres per second in each second, or $20 \, \text{m/s}^2$. The average acceleration corresponds to the gradient of a chord of the velocity-time graph. The acceleration of a moving body at a particular instant corresponds to the gradient of the tangent to the velocity-time graph at that instant.

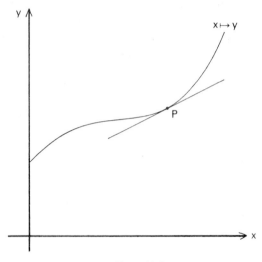

Figure 12.6

Using the language of rates, velocity is the rate of change of displacement, and acceleration is the rate of change of velocity. In general if a graph of a function $f : x \mapsto y$ is drawn, the gradient of the tangent at P corresponds to the rate of change of y with respect to x at P. Very often when we talk of a rate of change it is a rate of change with respect to time which is meant, and in this case the phrase "with respect to time" is often omitted.

12.4. Remarks

This is a convenient stopping point for a school course and the *SMP* course and some other courses go no further than this towards calculating either areas or gradients without approximations being made en route. Pupils who have reached this stage are well prepared for integration and differentiation, and in addition they will understand clearly why integration and differentiation are important processes.

While pupils are drawing tangents by eye, brief informal discussion of drawing methods can help to form ideas which will be useful in calculating gradients of curves without drawing. Pupils use two methods.

(i) The ruler is slid up to the curve, its direction being adjusted by eye until it approximates to the direction of the curve at the required point P.

(ii) The pencil is placed at P and the ruler slid round from a position such as PQ to a position where the second

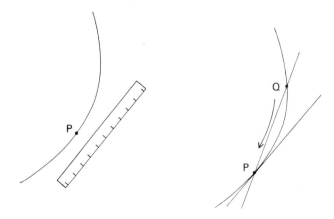

Figure 12.7   Methods of drawing tangents by eye.

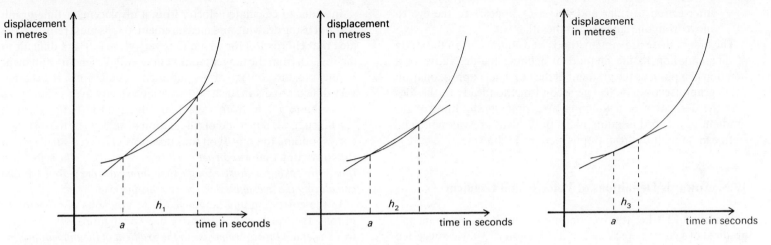

Figure 12.8   Average velocity over a short time interval.

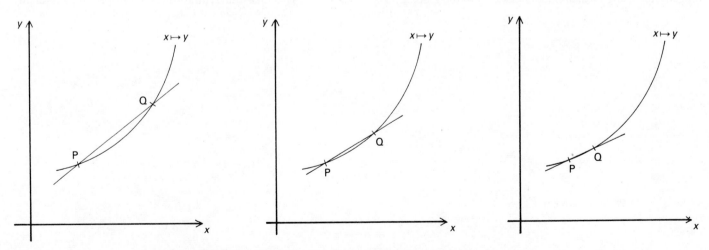

Figure 12.9   Approximations to the gradient of a tangent.

intersection of ruler and curve, Q, appears to the eye to move from one side of P to the other.

The first of these drawing methods leads ultimately in the study of differentiation to the method of defining the derivative of a function at a point as the gradient of the best linear approximation to its graph (section 14.5). The second method leads to the idea that the derivative of a function at a point is the limit of the gradient of a chord (section 14.3). Both ideas are valuable, and both can be built up from pupils' actions in drawing.

12.5. Towards Definitions of Velocity and Gradient

In section 12.2 the intuitive concepts of velocity at an instant and gradient of a curve were linked, and in section 12.3 it was suggested that pupils should do plenty of numerical examples in which they draw a tangent line to a curve and then calculate the gradient of the tangent line using measurements made from the graph.

In order to calculate velocity from a displacement-time graph without using drawing and measurement, pupils must return to the idea that chords PQ for which Q is very close to P are difficult to distinguish from the tangent to the curve at P. When this statement is put into the context of displacement-time graphs, it becomes very difficult to distinguish "the average velocity over a short time interval a to $a + h$" from the actual velocity at P (figure 12.8).

This suggests a method of calculation of velocity at the instant a corresponding to point P on the curve, for it is now a small step to the conviction that *we can get as close as we please to the velocity at time* a *by taking a short enough time interval from* a *to* $a+h$ *and calculating the average velocity over this interval.*

In the corresponding language about gradients of tangents to graphs, the words in italics above become (figure 12.9).
we can get as close as we please to the gradient of the tangent at P by taking Q close enough to P and calculating the gradient of the chord PQ.

This idea, differentiation, is developed in chapter 14.

13 The Definite Integral

13.1. Introduction

In chapter 11, the idea that the area under a velocity-time graph gives a measure of displacement was discussed; it was also indicated that the areas under other graphs can give useful information. This chapter discusses methods of calculating areas under the graphs of functions, and so introduces the definite integral.

Textbooks for pupils under sixteen vary considerably in their treatment of integration. Some do not consider it at all, others start with anti-differentiation while yet others emphasize area. None of these books uses the calculator, which will greatly influence the teaching of integration in the next few years.

Most pupils at present first meet integration as the reverse of differentiation, and only later do they use integrals to calculate areas. The authors believe that this approach gives pupils a very wrong impression conceptually, and is at variance with the way in which integration developed historically.

In the next sections we present a possible way of teaching integration to beginners, based on the use of calculators, area and summation. The treatment is independent of ideas about gradient and differentiation. Pupils may or may not be developing ideas which lead to differentiation in parallel with those which lead to the definite integral, but they will certainly not suspect at this stage that the calculation of areas and the calculation of gradients are related problems. In later work, in the sixth form, the fact that a definite integral is calculated by summation becomes increasingly important, for it enables applied mathematicians, statisticians and others to use integration in order to calculate such quantities as centres of gravity, moments of inertia, means and standard deviations.

In the sections which follow elementary and pictorial arguments are used to convince pupils that

$$\int_a^t x^p \, dx = \frac{t^{p+1}}{p+1} - \frac{a^{p+1}}{p+1}$$

provided, of course, that $p \neq -1$. A pictorial demonstration of

$$\int_a^t \lambda f(x) \, dx = \lambda \int_a^t f(x) \, dx$$

where λ is a fixed real number is given, and a similar demonstration of

$$\int_a^t (f(x) + g(x)) \, dx = \int_a^t f(x) \, dx + \int_a^t g(x) \, dx$$

may be given, so that a variety of elementary functions can be integrated.

13.2. Areas and Sandwiches

The problem is to calculate the area under the graph shown in figure 13.1(i), and the only knowledge required is that of the area of a rectangle. The procedure is the same as that described in chapter 11, when a "fast man" and "slow man" were introduced. In this case the interval on the x-axis from a to t is divided into n parts, and two step-functions, the *lower step-function* shown in figure 13.1(ii) and the *upper step-function* of figure 13.1(iii), are constructed. A sandwich argument can then be used.

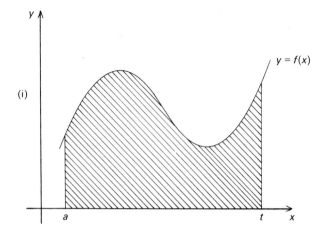

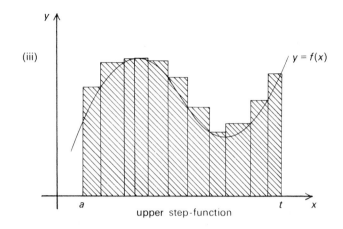

Figure 13.1   (i) Area under the graph of $y = f(x)$; (ii) lower step-function; (iii) upper step-function.

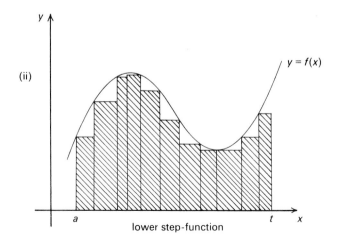

For simple functions, numerical calculations are very quickly made, as the following examples show.

We first find a sandwich inequality for the area under the graph of $y = x^2$ between $x = 0$ and $x = 1$, using lower and upper step-functions with ten steps each of width 0·1. Figure 13.2 shows the lower step-function.

The sandwich inequality is

$$0·285 \leqslant \text{area} \leqslant 0·385$$

and is obtained very quickly indeed. (A calculator is more hindrance than help!)

A calculator is more help if the inequality is refined by taking a step-function with twenty steps each of width 0·05. This time the sandwich inequality is

$$0·30875 \leqslant \text{area} \leqslant 0·35875$$

If an approximation is made to the area under the graph by averaging the upper and lower estimates (see section 7.3) the result is 0·33375. Hence, to 2 decimal places, an estimate of the area under

$y = x^2$ between $x = 0$ and $x = 1$ is 0·33, but a clear distinction must be drawn between the inequality which is *precise* and the average result which is *approximate*.

This work can be followed up by using similar approximate methods to calculate areas under the graphs of $y = x^3$ and $y = x^4$ between $x = 0$ and $x = 1$.

The table below gives approximate results, using ten-step step-functions, for the areas under the graphs of $y = x^p$ for $p = 0, 1, 2, \ldots, 9$. The step-function areas are omitted for $p = 0$ and $p = 1$ because the required areas are those of a rectangle and a triangle and can be calculated directly. In these cases the number in the right-hand column is the actual area under the graph.

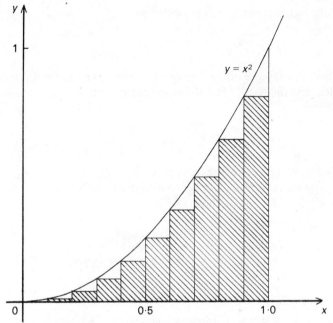

Figure 13.2   A lower step-function for the graph of $y = x^2$.

Value of p	Equation of graph	Area under lower step-function	Area under upper step-function	Average of the lower step-function area and upper step-function area (to two decimal places)
0	$y = 1$	—	—	1
1	$y = x$	—	—	0·5
2	$y = x^2$	0·285	0·385	0·33
3	$y = x^3$	0·2025	0·3025	0·25
4	$y = x^4$	0·1533	0·2533	0·20
5	$y = x^5$	0·1208	0·2208	0·17
6	$y = x^6$	0·0978	0·1978	0·15
7	$y = x^7$	0·0808	0·1808	0·13
8	$y = x^8$	0·0677	0·1677	0·12
9	$y = x^9$	0·0574	0·1574	0·11

The sequence of approximations in the right-hand column is

$$1, 0·5, 0·33, 0·25, 0·20, 0·17, \ldots$$

and suggests very strongly that the actual areas are

$$1, \tfrac{1}{2}, \tfrac{1}{3}, \tfrac{1}{4}, \tfrac{1}{5}, \tfrac{1}{6}, \ldots$$

This is not a proof, but it is a very convincing demonstration to pupils at this stage that the area under $y = x^p$ between $x = 0$ and $x = 1$ is $1/(p+1)$.

It is suggested that the numerical verification of this result, given above, is sufficient for almost all pupils, and a formal theoretical proof should be postponed to the next stage of work.

13.3. Definition of the Definite Integral

The definite integral of a function f between a and t can now be introduced as the area under the graph of $y = f(x)$ between $x = a$

and $x = t$, where $t \geqslant a$. It is written as

$$\int_a^t f(x)\,dx$$

Thus, the definite integral is merely a new notation for a familiar idea, and the result obtained at the end of section 13.2 can now be written

$$\int_0^1 x^p\,dx = \frac{1}{p+1}$$

where p is a positive integer or zero.

The same formula can be verified quite easily when $p = \frac{1}{2}$ and $p = \frac{1}{3}$, by the same method.

Value of p	Integral required	Area under lower step-function	Area under upper step-function	Average	$\dfrac{1}{p+1}$
$\frac{1}{2}$	$\displaystyle\int_0^1 x^{1/2}\,dx$	0·6105	0·7105	0·66	0·67
$\frac{1}{3}$	$\displaystyle\int_0^1 x^{1/3}\,dx$	0·6874	0·7874	0·74	0·75

It will now seem very justifiable to pupils that

$$\int_0^1 x^p\,dx = \frac{1}{p+1}$$

for all rational numbers $p \geqslant 0$.

The curious notation $\int f(x)\,dx$ often gives rise to comments and queries. Pupils may be told that δx is a common notation for the width of each strip, so that if m is the height of the lower step-function on that strip and M the height of the upper step-function on the same strip, we have

$$m\delta x \leqslant \text{area of strip} \leqslant M\delta x.$$

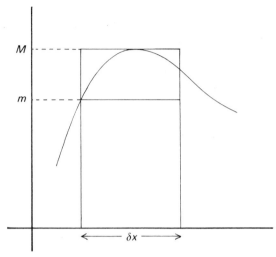

Figure 13.3

Hence

$$\Sigma m\delta x \leqslant \text{area under graph} \leqslant \Sigma M\delta x$$

where $\Sigma m\delta x$ may be read as "the sum of all the terms like $m\delta x$". Moreover, the values of $f(x)$ on the strip lie between m and M, so that the inequality now reads

$$\Sigma m\delta x \leqslant \int_a^t f(x)\,dx \leqslant \Sigma M\delta x$$

and $\int$ can be regarded as another form of the summation sign.

The notation for integrals certainly needs further discussion at the next stage, when use will be made of definite integrals to handle limits of sums, for instance when studying the mean and standard deviation of a continuous distribution.

13.4. Integrals of Increasing Functions

By this stage, pupils should have realized intuitively that if they make the steps of the step-functions narrower, they make the sandwich inequality thinner. Indeed for all the graphs so far considered the thickness of the sandwich inequality, or the difference between the upper step-function area and the lower step-function area, is of the form shown by the shaded area in figure 13.4. All these areas can be slid over to the left and stacked into the column shown against the y-axis. If the steps all have equal width w, the shaded area is $w \times 1 = w$. Hence the sandwich can be made *as thin as we please by* choosing w small enough.

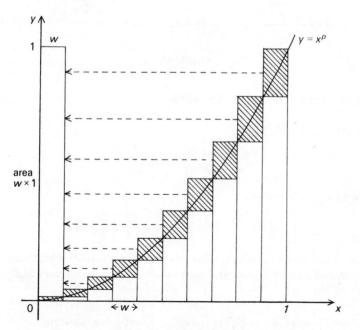

Figure 13.4   Difference between the upper and lower step-functions for $y = x^p$.

From the sandwich assumption of section 9.7, there is just one number which is sandwiched between every possible lower step-function area and every possible upper step-function area, and we can, by making the steps of our step-function sufficiently narrow, identify this number.

This argument applies not only to the integral of $y = x^p$ between 0 and 1, but to every increasing function because the shaded areas can always be stacked. Hence every increasing function has a definite integral which can be evaluated by a sandwiching process; so also do decreasing functions.

Pupils under sixteen will not concern themselves with the details of this argument, but the intuition that smaller step-lengths give a thinner sandwich should be encouraged. Later, more-advanced students will prove that not only every increasing function, but also every continuous function (and some other functions as well) has a definite integral which can be evaluated by a sandwiching process.

13.5. Extending the Result

Having assumed that

$$\int_0^1 x^p \, dx = \frac{1}{p+1} \quad \text{for} \quad p \geqslant 0$$

we can now use the sandwich method of the previous section to show that

$$\int_0^t x^p \, dx = \frac{t^{p+1}}{p+1}$$

Pupils should, however, have the opportunity to explore the result for themselves by some more summation exercises before meeting the following demonstration. We consider a lower step-function which has been used to arrive at the result

$$\int_0^1 x^p\,dx = \frac{1}{p+1}$$

A typical step is shown in figure 13.5. The step is of width w and starts at a, so its height is a^p. To obtain a step-function which is helpful for the integral from 0 to t, we stretch the set of steps in the x-direction with scale-factor t, so that they occupy the space from $x = 0$ to $x = t$. The steps are also stretched in the y-direction so that they still form a lower step-function for $y = x^p$. This is shown in figure 13.5(ii); the height of the step shown is $(at)^p$. Thus the width of the typical step is multiplied by t, and its height by t^p, so its area is multiplied by t^{p+1}.

Each step-function used in obtaining a sandwich inequality for

$$\int_0^1 x^p\,dx$$

could be transformed in the same way, so

$$\int_0^t x^p\,dx = t^{p+1}\int_0^1 x^p\,dx = \frac{t^{p+1}}{p+1}.$$

By a simple subtraction argument we find that

$$\int_u^t x^p\,dx = \frac{t^{p+1}}{p+1} - \frac{u^{p+1}}{p+1}.$$

The notation $[F(x)]_u^t$ can now be introduced as an abbreviation for $F(t) - F(u)$.

Hence

$$\int_u^t x^p\,dx = \left[\frac{x^{p+1}}{p+1}\right]_u^t = \frac{t^{p+1}}{p+1} - \frac{u^{p+1}}{p+1}$$

whenever $p \geqslant 0$ and p is rational.

This formula still holds when p is negative ($p \neq -1$) and pupils can verify it numerically if they wish.

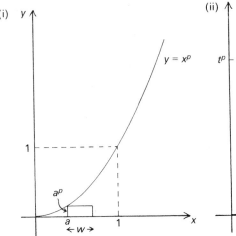
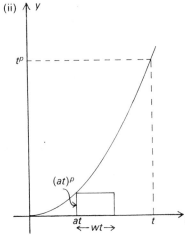

Figure 13.5

13.6. Integration of Polynomials

An integral such as

$$\int_0^2 (3x^2 + 2x)\,dx$$

has to be written as

$$\int_0^2 (3x^2 + 2x)\,dx = 3\int_0^2 x^2\,dx + 2\int_0^2 x\,dx$$

before it can be evaluated. This relies on two formulae which may be assumed for the present. These formulae, which look very likely to be true, are

$$\int_a^t \lambda f(x)\,dx = \lambda \int_a^t f(x)\,dx, \qquad \text{where } \lambda \text{ is a constant,}$$

and

$$\int_a^t (f(x)+g(x))\,dx = \int_a^t f(x)\,dx + \int_a^t g(x)\,dx.$$

Using these formulae, all the usual exercises involving the calculation of areas under graphs of polynomials can be tackled.

Numerical experiment with lower and upper step-functions for integrals such as

$$\int_0^1 3x^2\,dx \quad \text{and} \quad \int_0^1 (x^2+x)\,dx$$

will rapidly convince pupils of the truth of the formulae. If desired, the exploration of step-functions can easily be refined to demonstrate the two formulae, in the way shown below.

In figure 13.6, the graphs of $y = f(x)$ and $y = \lambda f(x)$ are shown for a value of λ which is about $1\frac{1}{2}$. In the two graphs, the corresponding steps of the step-functions have equal widths, and the height of each step in diagram (i) is multiplied by λ to give the height of the corresponding step in diagram (ii). From (i) we know that

$$\begin{array}{ccccc} \text{lower step-function} & & \text{area under graph} & & \text{upper step-function} \\ \text{area for } f & \leqslant & \text{of } y = f(x) & \leqslant & \text{area for } f \end{array}$$

and hence, multiplying by λ^*, we obtain

$$\lambda\left(\begin{array}{c}\text{lower step-function} \\ \text{area for } f\end{array}\right) \leqslant \lambda\left(\begin{array}{c}\text{area under graph} \\ \text{of } y = f(x)\end{array}\right) \leqslant \lambda\left(\begin{array}{c}\text{upper step-function} \\ \text{area for } f\end{array}\right) \quad (1)$$

From (ii) we see that

$$\begin{array}{ccccc} \text{lower step-function} & & \text{area under graph} & & \text{upper step-function} \\ \text{area for } \lambda f & \leqslant & \text{of } y = \lambda f(x) & \leqslant & \text{area for } \lambda f \end{array}$$

---

* λ is assumed to be positive. There are minor adjustments to be made if λ is negative or zero.

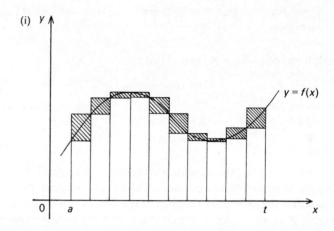

(i)

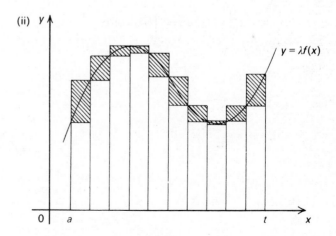

(ii)

Figure 13.6   Step-functions for $y = f(x)$ and $y = \lambda f(x)$.

or

$$\lambda\begin{pmatrix}\text{lower step-function}\\\text{area for } f\end{pmatrix} \leqslant \begin{matrix}\text{area under graph}\\\text{of } y = \lambda f(x)\end{matrix} \leqslant \lambda\begin{pmatrix}\text{upper step-function}\\\text{area for } f\end{pmatrix} \quad (2)$$

Combining inequalities (1) and (2) gives

$$\lambda\begin{pmatrix}\text{lower step-function}\\\text{area for } f\end{pmatrix}\begin{matrix}\leqslant \lambda\begin{pmatrix}\text{area under graph}\\\text{of } y = f(x)\end{pmatrix} \leqslant\\ \leqslant \quad \begin{matrix}\text{area under graph}\\\text{of } y = \lambda f(x)\end{matrix} \quad \leqslant\end{matrix}\lambda\begin{pmatrix}\text{upper step-function}\\\text{area for } f\end{pmatrix}$$

Now for $y = f(x)$, the sandwich inequality can be made as thin as we please by taking a step-function with thin enough steps, so it follows that the quantities outlined in the blocks can be made as close together as we please. We conclude that the middle terms of the two inequalities are equal.

Hence

$$\lambda \int_a^t f(x)\,dx = \int_a^t \lambda f(x)\,dx.$$

The second formula

$$\int_a^t (f(x)+g(x))\,dx = \int_a^t f(x)\,dx + \int_a^t g(x)\,dx$$

is demonstrated similarly.

13.7. Comments

In the above treatment, no reference is made to differentiation, so that the definite integral can be studied as an extension of the pupil's knowledge of area and sandwiching, independently of work on gradient and differentiation. In chapter 15 the link between the definite integral and differentiation is discussed.

It is suggested that this treatment establishes patterns of thought which are helpful to the future user of mathematics, whether he is a pure mathematician, applied mathematician, scientist, engineer, or economist.

14   Differentiation

14.1. Introduction

The *gradient* of the graph of a function at a point is the gradient of the tangent to the graph at that point. Traditionally, the method of calculating this has been to find the gradient of a chord PQ through point P, and then to find the *limit* of the gradient of PQ as Q approaches P (figure 14.1). We shall call this the *chord* approach

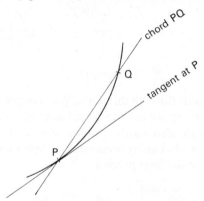

Figure 14.1

to differentiation. It was Newton's original method based on velocity and was used in almost all school textbooks published before 1960 which included any calculus.

The *SMP* "A" Level course pioneered another approach, using the geometrical picture of a function given by the arrow diagram. The ratio $\dfrac{L'M'}{LM}$, in the Cartesian graph of figure 14.2(i), measures the gradient of the chord PQ, but in the arrow diagram of figure

14.2(ii), the same ratio $\dfrac{L'M'}{LM}$ measures the *scale-factor* of the enlargement from LM to L'M'. The calculations are the same as in the chord approach, but because the geometrical interpretation is essentially different, we shall call this approach to differentiation the *scale-factor approach*.

In 1970, Montgomery and Jones, in *Calculus and Elementary Functions*, gave the first elementary treatment of a third approach to differentiation, that of the *best linear approximation*. This has, so far, received little attention in schools, although the treatment was intended for sixteen-year olds. The picture is again that of the Cartesian graph, but the idea used is that among all the possible straight lines drawn through the point P of the graph, there is one which approximates to the curve more closely than any other. This best straight-line approximation is the tangent at P.

In the next sections we discuss these three approaches and also mention briefly one or two other possibilities. Whatever approach is used, there are considerable notational difficulties, and these are also considered.

14.2. Chords: a Numerical Approach

It is suggested that, before the age of sixteen, the major emphasis should be on the idea of the gradient of a graph, with careful attention to clarity of concept and wording, and many simple numerical examples. Calculators make it possible for pupils easily and rapidly to calculate gradients of many chords PQ (figure 14.3) through a given point P, and to acquire a feeling for the relationship between the position of the second point Q (for fixed

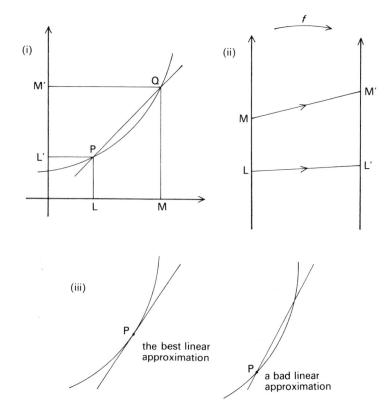

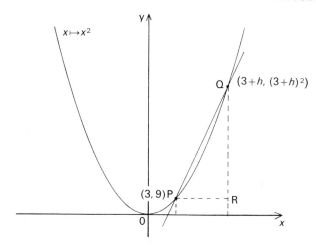

Figure 14.3

Figure 14.2 (i) Chord approach to differentiation; (ii) scale-factor approach to differentiation; (iii) best-linear-approximation approach to differentiation.

P) and the gradient of PQ. When the time comes for a more formal treatment, this numerical feeling for the gradient will help the pupil to understand what is going on behind the notation of limits.

For example, the gradient of the tangent to the graph of the function $x \mapsto x^2$ at the point $(3,9)$ can be approximated by finding

gradients of chords through this point. When pupils perform these calculations, they do not need to record as much as has been done below. They can also easily choose their own sequences of positions of Q, so that many numerical examples together give an understanding of the limit process.

x-coordinate of Q	y-coordinate of Q	QR	PR	Gradient of $PQ = \dfrac{QR}{PR}$
4	16	7	1	7
3·5	12·25	3·25	0·5	6·5
3·25	10·5625	1·5625	0·25	6·25
3·125	9·765625	0·765625	0·125	6·125
3·0625	9·37890625	0·37890625	0·0625	6·0625

The chords in this particular sequence have been chosen so that the x-distance of Q from P is continually halved. The sequence of gradients is

$$7, \; 6·5, \; 6·25, \; 6·125, \; 6·0625, \ldots$$

and it would seem that the gradient of the chord can be made *as close as we please to 6 by* taking Q close enough to P.

Another example of a sequence of chords PQ is the following, in which Q is on the left of P. Pupils should be encouraged to experiment with a variety of different positions of Q.

x-coordinate of Q	*y*-coordinate of Q	QR	PR	Gradient of PQ
2·9	8·41	−0·59	−0·1	5·9
2·99	8·9401	−0·0599	−0·01	5·99
2·999	8·994001	−0·005999	−0·001	5·999

Here again, it can be seen that we can make the gradient of the chord *as close as we please* to 6 by going far enough along the sequence of gradients

$$5·9, 5·99, 5·999, \ldots,$$

or by taking Q near enough to P.

It is the calculator which makes it easy for pupils to have personal experience of the process of finding gradients of sequences of chords through P. They can thus approximate to the gradient of the tangent through P by using chords whose intersections P and Q with the graph are very close together. Time spent in this numerical experimentation is well spent, for soon pupils will try to find positions of Q such that the gradient of PQ is within for instance 0·000001 of 6, and will realize that they cannot ever make the gradient of the chord PQ *exactly*,6. At this stage, the wording

the limit of the gradient of the chord as Q tends to P is 6

may be introduced to express the idea

the gradient of the chord can be made *as close as we please* to 6 by taking Q close enough to P.

When drawing diagrams such as that in figure 14.3, it is helpful to pupils' imagination to be sure that the chord is produced beyond P and Q, so that when P and Q are close together the chord is visible on the diagram, and can easily be related to the tangent at P.

14.3. Differentiation

In the numerical work, the same type of calculation has been repeated many times. The time has now come to generalize, and it will seem natural to find the gradient of the chord of $x \mapsto x^2$ joining $P(3,9)$ and $Q(3+h, (3+h)^2)$. Because P and Q are distinct points, h cannot be zero (see diagram opposite).

Now

$$QR = (3+h)^2 - 9$$

and

$$PR = h,$$

so the gradient of chord PQ is

$$\frac{QR}{PR} = \frac{(3+h)^2 - 9}{h}$$

$$= \frac{9 + 6h + h^2 - 9}{h}$$

$$= 6 + h.$$

As P and Q must be different points, *we can never have h = 0*, but the gradient of the chord PQ can be made as *close as we please* to 6 by taking h close enough to 0. It is important that pupils realize that although there is no chord whose gradient is exactly 6, there is a line through P whose gradient is exactly 6, and it is this line which is the tangent at P.

After this method of finding the gradient of the tangent at a point with given numerical coordinates, the next step is to generalize to find a rule for the gradient of the tangent to a graph of a function at

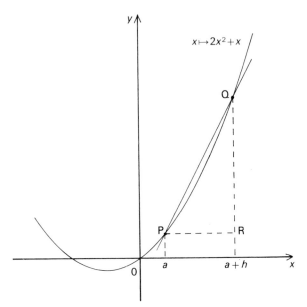

Figure 14.4

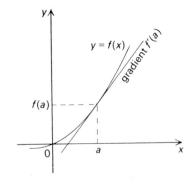

Figure 14.5

an arbitrary point P. The discussion given below is sufficiently simple to be within the grasp of pupils who have done the same thing numerically.

We shall find the gradient of the tangent to the graph of the function $x \mapsto 2x^2 + x$ at the point P, whose coordinates are $(a, 2a^2 + a)$. Since P is a given point, a is a fixed number throughout this calculation. We take a point Q on the graph *other than* P. The point Q is $(a+h, 2(a+h)^2 + (a+h))$ where h may be positive or negative, but is not zero.

The gradient of PQ is $\dfrac{\mathrm{QR}}{\mathrm{PR}}$, and

$$\frac{\mathrm{QR}}{\mathrm{PR}} = \frac{2(a+h)^2 + (a+h) - 2a^2 - a}{h}$$

$$= \frac{4ah + 2h^2 + h}{h}$$

$$= 4a + 2h + 1.$$

The gradient of the chord can be made as close as we please to $4a+1$ by taking h close enough to 0. Hence the gradient of the tangent at P is $4a+1$.

When this is thoroughly grasped, the teacher may wish to introduce the notation

$$\lim_{h \to 0} (4a + 2h + 1) = 4a + 1$$

but this is unnecessary and can be harmful to beginners, for it suggests to the pupil that he is putting $h = 0$. It seems better to expect pupils to say to themselves

the gradient of the chord can be made as close as we please to $4a+1$ by taking h close enough to 0, so the gradient of the tangent is $4a+1$.

The next notational step is

If $f(x) = 2x^2 + x$, then $f'(a) = 4a + 1$.

using $f'(a)$ to symbolize the gradient or *derivative* of the function f at the point a in just the same way that $f(a)$ is used to symbolize the value of the function at the point a (figure 14.5).

However, notation should not be forced upon pupils who have not absorbed the ideas. It is quite satisfactory at this stage if they express the gradient of a graph in words such as

the gradient of $x \mapsto 2x^2 + x$ at a is $4a + 1$.

The notations δx, δy and $\dfrac{dy}{dx}$ are better avoided until later, for a number of reasons:

(i) The symbols δx and δy are the pupils' first experience of using two letters to stand for a single number.

The temptation is strong to think of δx as a multiple of x, and δy as the same multiple of y, so that pupils may want to write $\dfrac{\delta y}{\delta x} = \dfrac{y}{x}$, in the same way that $\dfrac{\pi y}{\pi x} = \dfrac{y}{x}$. This notational problem has to be faced at some time, but a time when pupils are meeting several other new and subtle ideas is not the best time for extra notational difficulties.

(ii) In the traditional notation shown in figure 14.6, the symbol x is used with two quite distinct meanings, as can be seen from the two occurrences of x on the horizontal axis. It is first the x-coordinate of an *arbitrary* point on the graph $y = x^2$ of the function $f : x \mapsto x^2$. Secondly, it is the x-coordinate of a *particular* point P on the graph, and so is a fixed number. It can only be used for both by an abuse of notation which is very unsuitable until a later stage.

This confusion is easily avoided by using a letter other than x for the x-coordinate of P. Then we may say that, since $f'(a) = 2a$ for each point a, we have established a new function, the *derived*

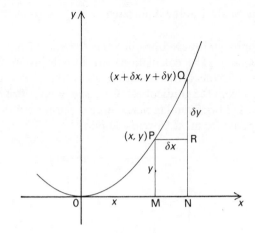

Figure 14.6

function f', which is given by $f'(x) = 2x$ for all x. The traditional notation

$$\frac{dy}{dx} = 2x \quad \text{for all } x$$

can then be introduced, but this notation has no advantages for pupils before sixteen.

In many "O" Level texts in which differentiation is treated, the aim seems to be the achievement of rote learning of the formulae which enable pupils to differentiate expressions such as $3x^2 - \dfrac{2}{x^3}$.

This is not a suitable aim if it is done at the expense of the understanding of how gradients of graphs are found. In the first treatment of differentiation, attention should be focused on methods rather than on formulae.

14.4. The Scale-Factor Approach

This approach is developed in *SMP Revised Advanced Mathematics, Book 1*. The calculations are exactly as in the chord approach, but the arrow diagram gives a different geometric motivation from the gradient of a Cartesian graph. The method is now discussed briefly in language more sophisticated than would be appropriate for most 16-year-old pupils.

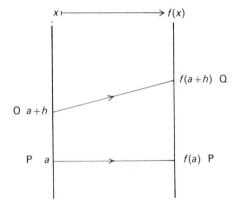

Figure 14.7

The closed interval $PQ[a, a+h]$ of the domain is considered. This interval is mapped so that P maps to P' and Q maps to Q'. The signed lengths P'Q' and PQ are then calculated and found to be $f(a+h)-f(a)$ and h respectively. The quotient

$$\frac{f(a+h)-f(a)}{h}, \quad \text{which is} \quad \frac{P'Q'}{PQ},$$

with attention paid to signs, is calculated and called the *average*

scale-factor over the interval PQ. The idea of *local scale-factor* at P is introduced, so that

$$\lim_{h \to 0} \frac{f(a+h)-f(a)}{h}$$

is interpreted as the local scale-factor of the function at P.

One or two difficulties occur in this interpretation. The first arises when a point between P and Q maps to a point which is not

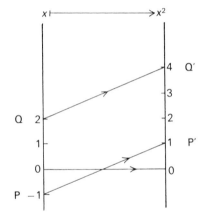

Figure 14.8

between P' and Q'. This happens in the case of the function $x \mapsto x^2$, when we consider the interval $[-1, 2]$. Because 0 maps to 0, the whole interval $[-1, 2]$ does not map to the interval $[1, 4]$; it is P which maps to P' and Q which maps to Q', not PQ which maps to P'Q'. The idea of scale-factor is geometrically more obscure in this example.

The other pictorial difficulty is that the local scale-factor can never actually be seen because it cannot be drawn. It literally almost vanishes as the interval PQ becomes small.

These difficulties are greater than those which occur in the gradient approach, in which the expression $\dfrac{f(a+h)-f(a)}{h}$ always represents the gradient of a chord. Even when h is very close to zero, the gradient of the extended chord is visible in the diagram, and the extended chord is almost indistinguishable from the tangent.

The authors of *SMP Revised Advanced Mathematics* must have been aware of these difficulties, for they introduce the gradient picture very soon after differentiation has been defined using scale-factor ideas, and with one exception subsequent work in *Revised Advanced Mathematics I* is all based on the gradient-of-chord picture rather than the scale-factor picture.

This exception is the rule for differentiating composite functions (or the chain rule), which has a very natural interpretation using scale-factors but no equivalent easy picture using gradients. The quotation below is taken from *Revised Advanced Mathematics I*, and is given to show the use of the scale-factor approach at the next stage of work. By this time, this text has introduced the traditional δx and δy notation (*SMP Revised Advanced Mathematics, Book I*, p. 305).

2.3 Alternative statement of the chain rule. Using the notation shown in Figure 7, the average scale factor of the function $f : x \to y$ over the interval of length δx is

$$\frac{\delta y}{\delta x} = \frac{\delta y}{\delta u} \times \frac{\delta u}{\delta x}.$$

To find the value of the derived function, dy/dx, we have to consider the limit as $\delta x \to 0$; $\delta y/\delta x \to dy/dx$, $\delta y/\delta u \to dy/du$ and $\delta u/\delta x \to du/dx$ so it would be reasonable to conclude that

$$\frac{dy}{dx} = \frac{dy}{du} \times \frac{du}{dx}.$$

To prove the result formally, which we shall not attempt here, we have to cope with the limit of a product and also the possibility that δu might be zero even if $\delta x \neq 0$. (What difficulty would this create?)

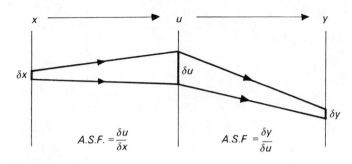

Fig. 7

It is interesting to note that the authors do not attempt to prove the result but make it clear that assumptions are made. This contrasts favourably with most texts, which claim to "prove" the chain rule, but take no account of the difficulties mentioned at the end of the extract.

It will be seen that the scale-factor picture forms a useful supplement to the gradient-of-chord picture, but cannot replace it.

14.5. The Best Linear Approximation

This approach is not well known, and so is described in some detail. The interested reader should consult Montgomery and Jones, *Calculus and Elementary Functions* (CUP) for a teaching method, and Fraleigh, *Calculus, A Linear Approach*, Vol. I (Addison Wesley) for a more advanced treatment.

The essential idea is that of trying to find a straight line which fits the graph of a function at a point better than any other straight line. This line (if it exists) is defined to be the tangent to the graph at the point (figure 14.9).

The equation of the tangent is also the equation of the best *linear* approximation to the function at that point. For example, when

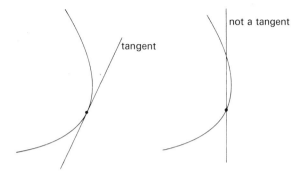

Figure 14.9

the values of the function $x \mapsto 2 + 3x + x^2$ are calculated near $x = 0$, it is found that the x^2-term makes little difference, compared with $2 + 3x$.

x	$2 + 3x$	$2 + 3x + x^2$
-1	-1	0
$-0\cdot1$	$1\cdot7$	$1\cdot71$
$-0\cdot001$	$1\cdot997$	$1\cdot997001$
0	2	2
$0\cdot001$	$2\cdot003$	$2\cdot003001$
$0\cdot1$	$2\cdot3$	$2\cdot31$
1	5	6

Thus, for x near 0, the error in replacing $2 + 3x + x^2$ by $2 + 3x$ is small. Discussion of the interval of values of x for which the error is "acceptably" small is helpful. Moreover, the graph of $x \mapsto 2 + 3x$ is a straight line, where that of $x \mapsto 2 + 3x + x^2$ is a curve. The x^2-term can helpfully be regarded as the *error term* in replacing $2 + 3x + x^2$ by $2 + 3x$. When finding a best linear approximation near a particular point we always try to replace a non-linear function by a linear function such that the error is small in comparison with the linear function near the point. Graph drawing should convince pupils that the graph of $x \mapsto 2 + 3x$ is the tangent to $x \mapsto 2 + 3x + x^2$ at $(0, 2)$.

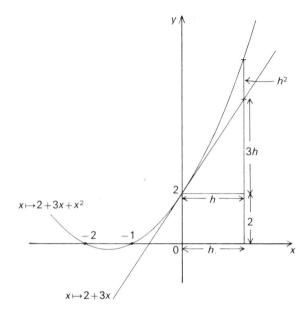

Figure 14.10

It is essential that pupils should understand from numerical experience that *near 0, x^2 is small in comparison with x*, so that the terms $2 + 3x$ dominate. Figure 14.10 shows the geometrical significance of the three terms at the point $x = h$.

The derivative of the function when $x = 0$ can now be calculated as the gradient of the best linear approximation near $x = 0$. Thus, the derivative of $x \mapsto 2 + 3x + x^2$ at $x = 0$ is 3.

This approach is easily adapted when the derivative at a point other than $x = 0$ is required, as the following numerical example shows. We try to find the derivative of the function

$$x \mapsto 3 - 3x + x^2 - x^3 \quad \text{at} \quad x = 2.$$

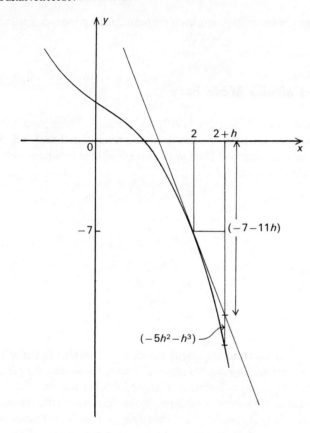

Figure 14.11

We consider the point $x = 2 + h$, at which

$$3 - 3x + x^2 - x^3 = 3 - 3(2 + h) + (2 + h)^2 - (2 + h)^3$$

$$= 3 - 6 - 3h + 4 + 4h + h^2 - 8 - 12h - 6h^2 - h^3$$

$$= -7 - 11h - 5h^2 - h^3.$$

Again, numerical experiment and graph drawing will be needed to convince pupils that

(i) $-5h^2 - h^3$ can be made as small as we please in comparison with h by taking h near enough to 0,

(ii) the plotted values of $-7 - 11h$ give a straight line of gradient -11. This straight line fits the curve extremely closely at $x = 2$, and -11 is the derivative of the function at $x = 2$.

The teacher will realize that the substitution $x = 2 + h$ has merely moved the origin to $x = 2$, but pupils will not be accustomed to seeing the equation of a straight line in the form $y = -7 - 11h$, where $x = 2 + h$.

Numerical comparisons between $-7 - 11h$ and $3 - 3x + x^2 - x^3$ in the neighbourhood of $x = 2$ (or $h = 0$), will be helpful in enabling pupils to realize the accuracy of the linear approximation.

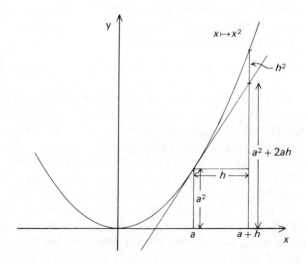

Figure 14.12

x	h	$-7-11h$	$3-3x+x^2-x^3$
2	0	-7	-7
2·1	0·1	$-8·1$	$-8·151$
2·01	0·01	$-7·11$	$-7·110501$
2·001	0·001	$-7·011$	$-7·011005$

More generally, for the function $f : x \mapsto x^2$, at the point $x = a$, we have (figure 14.12)

$$f(a+h) = a^2 + 2ah + h^2$$

and since h^2 can be made as small as we please in comparison with h by taking h close enough to 0, the best linear approximation is $h \mapsto a^2 + 2ah$, which has gradient $2a$. Hence $f'(a) = 2a$.

This way of introducing the derivative of a function at a point is easy and intuitive for polynomial functions. Its theoretical problems lie at the next stage, when *as small as we please in comparison with h* needs to be made precise. This is, however, no more difficult than in the traditional method, for the function f is defined to be differentiable at a and to have derivative A at that point if $f(a+h)$ can be written in the form

$$f(a+h) = f(a) + Ah + \eta h$$

where the error term is written as a multiple ηh of h, and can be made as small as we please in comparison with h by taking h small enough. For this to happen, we must be able to make η as close to 0 as we please by taking h near enough to 0.

The best-linear-approximation method is the only one which generalizes to higher dimensions, and so is the most useful in advanced work. There is at present insufficient experience of using it at the pre-"O" Level stage to know how effective it is as an introduction to differentiation, but certainly the calculations are extremely easy, so that they do not interfere with the comprehension of the ideas if the work is confined to polynomial functions. However, for pupils under the age of 16, confining the work to polynomial functions is recommended whatever approach is used.

14.6. *Calculus Made Easy*

In *Calculus Made Easy* (1910), Sylvanus P. Thompson talked without rigour about 'differentials' and maintained that if dx is a small enough increase, then $(dx)^2$ is negligible in comparison with dx. He then wrote

$$y = x^2$$

$$y + dy = (x + dx)^2$$

$$= x^2 + 2x \cdot dx$$

so

and

$$dy = 2x \cdot dx$$

$$\frac{dy}{dx} = 2x.$$

This is not a valid argument but methods similar to these have always been used by mathematicians and scientists as a way to find results which they subsequently prove by other means.

In 1961, however, Abraham Robinson was able to make rigorous an approach to calculus through infinitesimals. Robinson's work is known as *non-standard analysis*, and the first introductory calculus book making use of the ideas of non-standard analysis has recently appeared: H. J. Keisler, *Elementary Calculus* (Prindle, Weber & Schmidt, 1976). While Keisler's text is clearly unsuitable for pupils under sixteen, it may be that further work will produce greater simplification. Further development in the introduction of differentiation to beginners along these lines is possible in the next few years.

14.7. The Black-Box Technique

This technique for teaching differentiation admits that differentiation is difficult; therefore the teacher explains to the pupils that in the seventeenth century, Newton and Leibniz discovered that for a graph of the form $y = x^n$, the gradient is given by the formula nx^{n-1}.

While no self-respecting teacher admits to using this method, the effects of other methods presented with insufficient time and preparation are equivalent to a black box plus hang-ups on the part of the student, while the black-box method as described leaves a mystery but no hang-up about it!

14.8. The Derivative of $x \mapsto x^n$

For some pupils who have learnt to differentiate combinations of functions such as $x \mapsto x^2$ and $x \mapsto x^3$, the teacher may wish to proceed as far as finding the derivative of the function with formula $f(x) = x^n$, where n is a positive integer.

Care needs to be taken in deciding whether to make this extension, for it is easy for pupils to lose the thread of the argument in a maze of algebraic symbols. Most texts find the derivatives of $x \mapsto x^2$, $x \mapsto x^3$ and $x \mapsto x^4$, and then draw out a general rule from the pattern of the results. At this level this is a satisfactory procedure which many teachers will wish to follow.

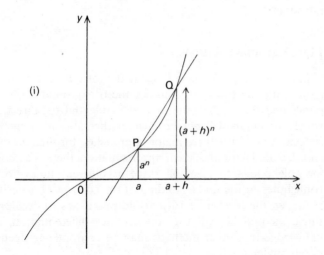

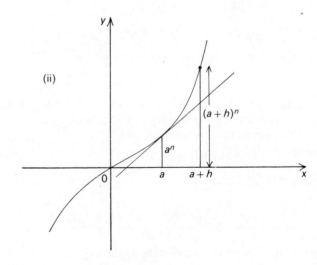

Figure 14.13   The derivative of $x \mapsto x^n$: (i) using Pascal's triangle; (ii) using the best-linear-approximation method.

Although it is not possible to give a rigorous proof that the gradient of $x \mapsto x^n$ at $x = a$ is na^{n-1} without using proof by induction somewhere in the chain of results, it is possible to use Pascal's Triangle to show a reason for the form of the result.

Pupils with skill at algebra can calculate

$$(a+h)^2 = a^2 + 2ah + h^2$$
$$(a+h)^3 = (a+h)(a^2 + 2ah + h^2)$$
$$= a^3 + 2a^2h + ah^2$$
$$\quad + a^2h + 2ah^2 + h^3$$
$$= a^3 + 3a^2h + 3ah^2 + h^3$$

and most of them will recognize that the coefficients form Pascal's Triangle

$a+h$			1		1	
$(a+h)^2$		1		2		1
$(a+h)^3$		1	3		3	1
$(a+h)^4$	1	4	6	4	1	

They can see from the pattern that $(a+h)^n$ starts

$$a^n + na^{n-1}h + \ldots,$$

but they find the formulae for later terms more difficult. However, formulae for these later terms are not necessary, and the calculation proceeds as follows (see figure 14.13):

The gradient of PQ

$$= \frac{(a+h)^n - a^n}{h}$$

$$= \frac{(a^n + na^{n-1}h + Aa^{n-2}h^2 + Ba^{n-3}h^3 + \ldots) - a^n}{h}$$

where $A, B, \ldots$ are later coefficients in the expansion of $(a+h)^n$. A and B have been used in order to avoid having to work out formulae. Thus, the gradient of PQ is

$$na^{n-1} + Aa^{n-2}h + Ba^{n-3}h^2 + \ldots.$$

This can be made *as close as we please to* na^{n-1} by taking h close enough to 0. The values of $A, B, \ldots$ do not matter.

It follows that the gradient of $x \mapsto x^n$ at $x = a$ is na^{n-1}. In other words,

$$\text{if} \quad f(x) = x^n, \quad \text{then} \quad f'(a) = na^{n-1}.$$

If the best-linear-approximation method is used, we consider the point $(a+h)$, at which $(a+h)^n = a^n + na^{n-1}h + Aa^{n-2}h^2 + \ldots$. The best linear approximation is $a^n + na^{n-1}h$, and this has gradient na^{n-1}.

No attempt should be made at this stage to show that the formula still holds when n is not a positive integer. Even in the case of a positive integer, a proof by induction will be given in the sixth form, but the search for a pattern given above forms a suitable introduction.

14.9. Recommendations

In considering how best to treat the introduction to differentiation, it is necessary to consider the backgrounds of both the pupils and the teacher, the time available and the directions in which the pupils will pursue their mathematics after the age of sixteen. Among the three major approaches, through gradient of chord, scale-factor and linear approximation, there is a good case for able pupils to meet all three at different times, for each contributes to the understanding of the concept of a derivative. However, the teacher of 16-year-old pupils has to decide which single method he will use to introduce differentiation, in the knowledge that other methods may be used later to deepen his pupils' understanding.

Notational problems also loom large. It has been suggested above that δx, δy and $\frac{dy}{dx}$ should not be used at this stage, because of the confusion between ideas inherent in them. However, if students' next encounter with calculus is to be in science or economics, they are very likely to be expected to use $\dfrac{dy}{dx}$, and should be aware of this notation and how it arises. Moreover, the $\delta x, \delta y, \dfrac{dy}{dx}$ notation has stood the test of 300 years' use, and many mathematicians think intuitively in terms of it; for instance the arc-length formula $\dfrac{ds}{dx} = \sqrt{1 + \left(\dfrac{dy}{dx}\right)^2}$ is remembered from

$$(\delta s)^2 \approx (\delta x)^2 + (\delta y)^2.$$

It seems clear that for most teachers, with most pupils, the gradient-of-chord approach will continue to be used (the scale-factor picture being helpful for composite functions) but there is a strong case for experiment with the best-linear-approximation approach. Innovative teachers may also like to consider non-standard analysis which, it is claimed by its American proponents, has improved understanding and performance in calculus at both school and college level.

15 Linking the Definite Integral with Differentiation

We have defined the definite integral as an area under a curve.

Thus $\int_a^b f(x)\,dx$ is the shaded area shown in figure 15.1.

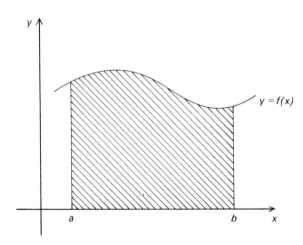

Figure 15.1   The definite integral as an area under a curve.

On the other hand, differentiation is linked to the gradient of a curve, a local scale-factor, or a best linear approximation.

The purpose of this chapter is to provide a link between the two concepts of the definite integral and the derivative which appear on the surface to be completely unrelated.

15.1. Which Comes First?

In this book, chapter 13 on the definite integral comes before the chapter on differentiation (chapter 14). In most school courses differentiation is tackled first and integration is subsequently introduced as the process of anti-differentiation. The treatment of integration given in chapter 13 does not depend on differentiation so, in order to give emphasis to this, it was put before differentiation. The fact that integration and differentiation are independent in the initial stages is crucial, and the authors believe that it is of great importance that they are taught independently and subsequently brought together by the fundamental theorem of the calculus which is discussed in this chapter.

This leaves open the question of whether integration should be taught before differentiation or not. The usual order in school is to teach differentiation first, but there are powerful arguments in favour of integration first. Some of these arguments for teaching the definite integral first are now discussed.

(i) As a general principle it is likely that when one thing is discovered before another it is simpler; more than a thousand years before anyone knew the methods of differentiation, Archimedes was finding definite integrals, as is shown in chapter 17.

(ii) The integral is a development of the idea of area, which has been well known to pupils since their primary-school days. Their first statistical graphs were made by using small squares to make a block graph or a histogram. Thus most pupils have been familiar with the concept of area for many years. On the other hand, at the age of sixteen, the idea of a rate is very recent to most pupils. Although a qualitative impression of steepness is plain in a graph, the measurement of gradient is by means of a *ratio*, and the understanding of ratio and proportion is found difficult by many pupils. Moreover, although pupils have drawn tangents to a graph by eye, and have calculated approximations to the gradient, formal differentiation is a much more complicated process.

(iii) An important mathematical argument for teaching the definite integral before differentiation is that it prevents integration being regarded first and foremost as the reverse of differentiation. Students can then see the fundamental theorem of calculus which links integration and differentiation for what it really is, a massive and surprising bridge linking the apparently independent mathematical structures of integration and differentiation.

(iv) Another advantage of teaching integration first is that it capitalizes on the certainty in the mind of the pupil that there really is a number which measures area. This is guaranteed by the sandwich theorem for the real numbers, which we have assumed, and which is intuitively obvious to pupils. The limit idea needed for finding the gradient of a tangent from the gradient of a chord is conceptually much harder.

(v) It is interesting that some attempts have been made to write books which present integration before differentiation, the most notable example being the first edition of *Modern Mathematics for Schools*. It is unfortunate that, in the second edition, the authors have reverted to putting differentiation first just at the time that the calculator eases the computation problems associated with the definite integral.

However, in the second edition of *Modern Mathematics for Schools*, the authors do carefully re-emphasize the independence of integration and differentiation.

15.2. The Link between Integration and Differentiation

To develop the link between integration and differentiation we need to appreciate that differentiation is a process applied to

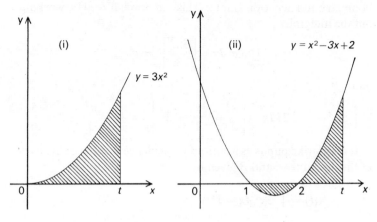

Figure 15.2

functions, whereas the definite integral is a *number*. We look for a function associated with an integral.

We consider integrals such as $\int_0^t 3x^2\,dx$ and $\int_1^t (x^2-3x+2)\,dx$ in which the lower limit is fixed and the upper limit may take any value. These integrals can be called *integral functions*, and it is necessary to ensure that pupils realize that these integrals depend on the value of t, and that x is a "dummy variable", which is only needed to tell us what graph we are finding the area under. Thus $\int_0^t 3x^2\,dx$ is the shaded area under $y = 3x^2$ in figure 15.2(i), and $\int_1^t (x^2-3x+2)\,dx$ is the shaded area under $y = x^2-3x+2$ in figure 15.2(ii) with sign taken into account. It is clear that $\int_0^t 3x^2\,dx$ and $\int_1^t (x^2-3x+2)\,dx$ depend on the position of the right-hand boundary and hence on t, not x. This can be reinforced by working out the integrals

$$\int_0^t 3x^2\, dx = \left[\frac{3x^3}{3}\right]_0^t = t^3$$

and

$$\int_1^t (x^2 - 3x + 2)\, dx = \left[\frac{x^3}{3} - \frac{3x^2}{2} + 2x\right]_1^t = \frac{t^3}{3} - \frac{3t^2}{2} + 2t - \frac{5}{6}$$

It may strike pupils as a curious coincidence that the derivatives of the functions A and B given by

$$A(t) = \int_0^t 3x^2\, dx = t^3$$

and

$$B(t) = \int_1^t (x^2 - 3x + 2)\, dx = \frac{t^3}{3} - \frac{3t^2}{2} + 2t - \frac{5}{6}$$

are

$$A'(t) = 3t^2 \quad \text{and} \quad B'(t) = t^2 - 3t + 2.$$

By drawing pictures of some integral functions such as A and B, finding their formulae and differentiating, pupils can be led to suggest the result that if a is a fixed number and

$$A(t) = \int_a^t f(x)\, dx$$

then

$$A'(t) = f(t).$$

Pupils will not realize that this result needs f to be continuous at t, but the time to discuss this point is in the sixth form, when a more formal proof can be given. However, even at this stage the work can go slightly beyond the feeling of surprise that integration and differentiation are linked, which the above algebraic work suggests.

15.3. Further Discussion of the Link between Integration and Differentiation

The reader may be worried by the fact that the work of the previous section relies on a statement which was assumed earlier on the basis of numerical evidence only. This statement is

$$\int_0^1 x^p\, dx = \frac{1}{p+1} \qquad (p \neq -1)$$

However, a link between derivatives and definite integrals may be made in another way, using three results from our knowledge of displacement-time and velocity-time graphs and the definition of an integral.

When a displacement-time graph is drawn for the motion of a particle, the velocity at each instant is the gradient of the graph at that instant (section 12.2). This is illustrated for time $t = T$ in figure 15.3(i).

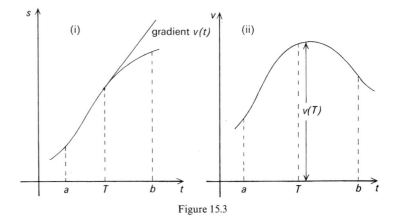

Figure 15.3

Pupils can plot the velocity-time graph for the motion of the same particle, by working out the gradient of the displacement-time graph at a number of points. In fact, at each time T,

$$v(T) = s'(T)$$

where $s'(T)$ is the derivative of s at time T. Hence v and s' are the same function of time.

Now it is also known (section 11.4) that the area under the velocity-time graph between $t = a$ and $t = b$ represents the displacement during that time; in symbols

$$\text{area under velocity-time graph} = s(b) - s(a).$$

The definite integral of a function is the area under its graph, so

$$\text{area under velocity-time graph} = \int_a^b v(t)\,dt$$

or

$$s(b) - s(a) = \int_a^b v(t)\,dt$$

$$= \int_a^b s'(t)\,dt$$

from the previous paragraph, using t as a place-holder instead of T.

Thus, for displacement and time, the formula

$$s(b) - s(a) = \int_a^b s'(t)\,dt$$

indicates that the definite integral between a and b of velocity, or the derivative of displacement, is the change in the displacement between a and b.

In order to get a more general result, we only have to move from s and t to y and x. This is easily done for a differentiable function in the following way.

Suppose the function $f:x \mapsto f(x)$ (figure 15.4) has a derivative at each point. Then certainly we can imagine a particle moving

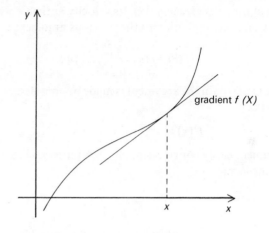

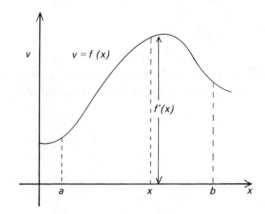

Figure 15.4

along a straight line in such a way that its displacement from the origin at time x is given by $f(x)$. Its velocity at time x will be $f'(x)$, and by an exact repetition of the previous argument we obtain

$$f(b) - f(a) = \int_a^b f'(x)\,dx.$$

The final step in the argument is made by considering a function f such that

$$f'(x) = x^p, \quad \text{where} \quad p \neq -1.$$

Experiment easily convinces pupils that the formula for $f(x)$ must be of the form

$$f(x) = \frac{x^{p+1}}{p+1} + c$$

where c is any real number. This immediately yields

$$\int_a^b x^p\,dx = \frac{b^{p+1}}{p+1} - \frac{a^{p+1}}{p+1} \quad (p \neq -1)$$

$$= \left[\frac{x^{p+1}}{p+1}\right]_a^b$$

Thus the link between the definite integral, defined as an area under a graph, and antidifferentiation is established.

This argument is suitable for able pupils who are sufficiently familiar with the relation between displacement-time and velocity-time graphs to argue from them. Proofs which do not depend on this fact are suitably left for the sixth form.

For the majority of pupils who meet the definite integral before the age of 16, the numerical verification of

$$\int_0^1 x^p\,dx = \frac{1}{p+1} \quad (p \neq -1)$$

carries complete conviction. If they regard the two facts

(i) $$\int_a^b x^p\,dx = \left[\frac{x^{p+1}}{p+1}\right]_a^b \quad (p \neq -1)$$

(ii) the derivative of $\left(\dfrac{x^{p+1}}{p+1}\right)$ is x^p $\quad (p \neq -1)$

as a curious coincidence, no harm will be done, for the first was studied for more than a thousand years before its connection with the second was discovered, as is shown in the final historical chapter of the book. More careful discussion of the connection between the two can appropriately wait for the next stage of the student's education.

16 Some Applications of Integration and Differentiation

The preceding two chapters were concerned with the calculation of areas and gradients, and neglected the applications which arise from integration and differentiation. In this chapter we discuss some examples of applications, while recognizing that teachers would want to introduce some of them during the teaching of integration and differentiation.

16.1. Displacement, Velocity and Acceleration

A particularly important example of the use of integration and differentiation occurs in the study of motion under gravity. It is found experimentally that when a heavy body falls in a vacuum under gravity, it falls with a constant acceleration. In real life, air resistance retards the fall, but the constant-acceleration model is very simple, and is often used. On the earth's surface the constant acceleration due to gravity is nearly $10 \, \text{m/s}^2$; that is, velocity increases by nearly 10 metres per second in each second.

It was seen in section 12.3 that the gradient of a velocity-time graph represents the rate of change of velocity with respect to time; this is called the *acceleration*. Thus, if a stone is allowed to fall from the top of a cliff, and the constant-acceleration model is used, the velocity-time graph is extremely simple, and has a constant gradient of 10. Thus, the equation of the velocity-time graph is

$$v = 10t$$

if we assume that the stone falls with zero initial velocity. Moreover, we also know that the area under the velocity-time graph represents the displacement, so that the displacement in T

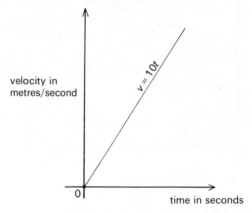

Figure 16.1   Velocity-time graph for a falling stone.

seconds is given by

$$
\begin{aligned}
s &= \int_0^T 10t \, dt \\
&= \left[5t^2 \right]_0^T \\
&= 5T^2.
\end{aligned}
$$

Thus, after T seconds, the stone has fallen $5T^2$ metres, and has a velocity of $10T \, \text{m/s}$.

In general, the velocity-time graph contains complete information about the motion of a body, for its gradient gives the acceleration at an instant, and the area under it represents the displacement up to that instant (figure 16.2).

A second example is that in which a ball is thrown *upwards* with initial velocity $5 \, \text{m/s}$. Here the acceleration is *downwards*, so the

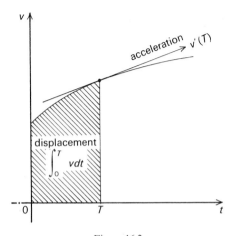

Figure 16.2

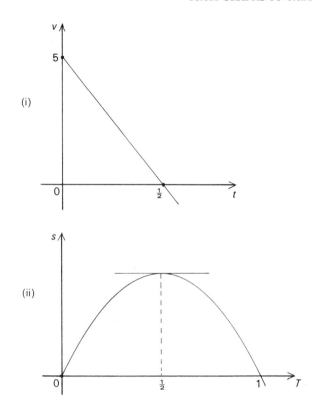

gradient of the velocity-time graph is $-10\,\text{m/s}^2$ (figure 16.3(i)).
After $\frac{1}{2}$ second, the ball changes from positive upward velocity
to negative upward velocity, and so starts to move down again.
The equation of the velocity-time graph is

$$v = 5 - 10t.$$

The *upward* displacement after T seconds is

$$s = \int_0^T (5 - 10t)\, dt$$
$$= 5T - 5T^2$$
$$= 5T(1 - T)$$

and the ball returns to the thrower's hand after 1 second. The
displacement-time graph is shown in figure 16.3(ii). Its point of
zero gradient occurs when $T = \frac{1}{2}$, and occurs at the instant at
which the velocity is zero.

Figure 16.3   (i) Velocity-time graph; (ii) displacement-time graph, for a ball
thrown upwards.

16.2. Graph Sketching

Pupils first become familiar with the shapes of the graphs of
well-known functions by numerical plotting of points. At that
stage every graph is a new experience, its shape unknown until a
number of points have been plotted.

It is an important stage in the development of the vocabulary of mathematics when pupils become explicitly aware of and can anticipate the shapes of the graphs of some basic functions.

It was suggested in chapter 6 that pupils by the age of sixteen should know (in numerical examples) that

(i) the graph of $y = mx + c$ is a straight line with gradient m,
(ii) the graph of $y = ax^2 + bx + c$ is a parabola.

They should also have plotted $y = \dfrac{1}{x}$, and have had some experience of plotting cubics.

For many purposes, however, it is not necessary to plot an accurate graph; skill at drawing a quick sketch which shows the major features of the graph of a function is useful when a graphical model is used, and should be beginning to develop by age sixteen.

Knowledge of how to calculate the gradient of a function from its equation is a considerable help in graph-sketching, and this knowledge should be used as soon as it is available.

Some examples will help to make the situation clear.

1. *Sketch the graph of the function $f : x \mapsto x^2 - 6x + 4$.*

(i) Pupils will expect the graph of this function to be a parabola whose vertex points either upwards or downwards. Large positive or negative values of x give rise to large positive values of $f(x)$, so the vertex of the parabola points down. It remains to locate the vertex.

The point $x = 0$, $y = 4$ is easily plotted as a control point. When $x = a$, the gradient of the graph is $2a - 6$. This indicates that the only point where the graph has zero gradient is given by

$$2a - 6 = 0$$

or

$$a = 3.$$

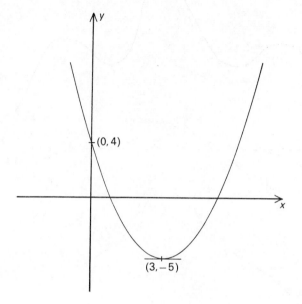

Figure 16.4　Sketch of the graph of $f : x \mapsto x^2 - 6x + 4$.

Thus, the vertex of the parabola is at $(3, -5)$.

(ii) Sometimes, the points at which $f(x) = 0$ are easily plotted. However, in this case, $f(x) = 0$ when

$$x^2 - 6x + 4 = 0$$

and the roots of the equation are irrational.

(iii) The sketch of the graph shown in figure 16.4 contains enough information for most purposes. Further confirmation can be obtained by noticing that the gradient, $2a - 6$, is positive when $a > 3$ and negative when $a < 3$.

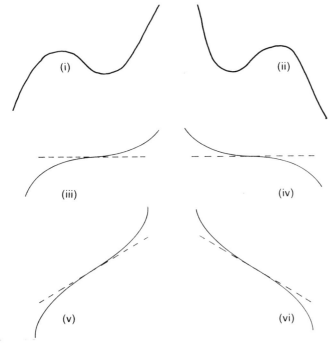

Figure 16.5   Shapes of the graphs of cubic functions.

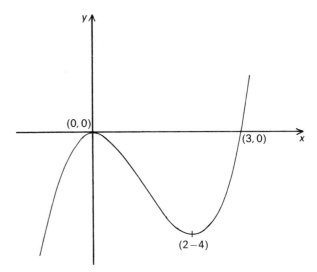

Figure 16.6   Sketch of the graph of $f : x \mapsto x^3 - 3x^2$.

2. *Sketch the graph of the function $f : x \mapsto x^3 - 3x^2$*

Previous experience of plotting graphs of cubic functions should lead pupils to expect a graph of one of the shapes shown in figure 16.5. The only problem is to decide which of these it is and to place it correctly with respect to the coordinate axes. Numerical experiment quickly satisfies pupils that when x is large (positive or negative), the term x^3 is more important than the term $-3x^2$, so that the sign of $f(x)$ is the same as the sign of x^3. When x is large and positive x^3 is large and positive. This restricts the shape to (i),

(iii) or (v); numerically large negative values of x confirm this. Substitution also shows that when $x = 0, f(x) = 0$, so $(0,0)$ lies on the graph. The gradient at $x = a$ is $f'(a) = 3a^2 - 6a$ and it can be seen that this is zero when $a = 0$ or 2; thus, the graph has two points of zero gradient, at $(0,0)$ and $(2, -4)$, and so is of type (i). In this case, it is easy to see what happens when $f(x) = 0$, and so where the graph meets the x-axis. At these points,

$$x^3 - 3x^2 = 0$$

and so $x = 0$ or $x = 3$. Thus the graph meets the x-axis at $(0,0)$ and $(3,0)$. The sketch in figure 16.6 shows all the main features of the graph.

The teacher may like to introduce vocabulary to describe the behaviour of the graph. The function is *increasing* when $x < 0$ and when $x > 2$; it is *decreasing* when $0 < x < 2$. Pupils should recognize that increasing functions have positive gradients, and decreasing functions have negative gradients. They know that the gradient when $x = a$ is

$$f'(a) = 3a^2 - 6a.$$

It is easily verified that, for instance,

when $a = -1, f'(a) = 9$;

when $a = 1, \quad f'(a) = -3$;

when $a = 3, \quad f'(a) = 9$.

The point of zero gradient at $(0,0)$ is a *local maximum*; the point of zero gradient at $(2, -4)$ is a *local minimum*.

Points of zero gradient are always either local maxima or minima, or horizontal points of inflexion, as shown in figure 16.7.

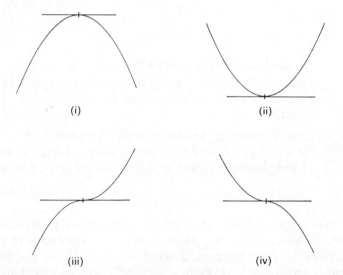

(i)   (ii)

(iii)   (iv)

Figure 16.7   Points of zero gradient: (i) local maximum; (ii) local minimum; (iii) horizontal points of inflexion.

At this stage, it is quite inappropriate for pupils to know rules, involving the second derivative, to distinguish between maxima, minima and points of inflexion. A sketch will nearly always suffice, and if any doubt remains, working out the gradient when x is just to the right or just to the left of the point of zero gradient will dispel all doubts.

3. *Sketch the graph of the function $f : x \mapsto 3x^5 - 20x^3$.*

This example is probably too advanced for all but the most-able pupils, but illustrates how much information about a graph points of zero gradient can give.

(i) $3x^5$ is the more important term, so when x is large and positive, $f(x)$ is large and positive; when x is large and negative, $f(x)$ is large and negative.

(ii) The gradient at $x = a$ is given by

$$f'(a) = 15a^4 - 60a^2.$$

Thus the points of zero gradient are at

$$15a^4 - 60a^2 = 0$$

or

$$15a^2(a^2 - 4) = 0.$$

Hence $a = 0, a = 2$ and $a = -2$ give points of zero gradient. These points are $(0,0)$, $(2, -64)$ and $(-2, 64)$. The information now known is shown in figure 16.8(i), and it is easy to complete the sketch, as in figure 16.8(ii).

If doubt remains, it is easy to check on the calculator that, for instance, the gradient at $a = 0.5$ is about -14, as is the gradient at $a = -0.5$.

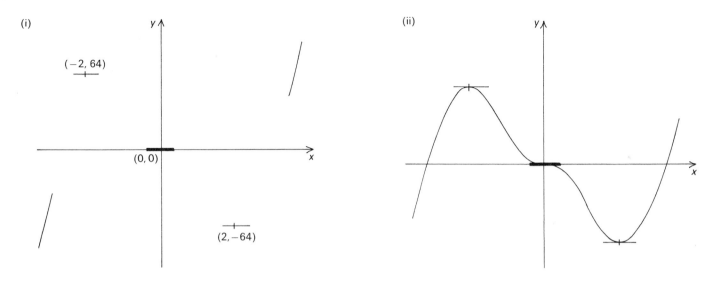

Figure 16.8   Sketch of the graph of $f : x \mapsto 3x^5 - 20x^3$.

4. *Sketch the graph of* $x \mapsto \dfrac{1}{x-1}$.

Although pupils will not be able to differentiate the function $x \mapsto 1/(x-1)$, they can draw a sketch showing the salient features of of the graph.

(i) For large positive values of x, the value of $\dfrac{1}{x-1}$ is very small but positive. For large negative values of x, the value of $\dfrac{1}{x-1}$ is very small and negative. The point $(0, -1)$ lies on the curve. This information is plotted immediately.

(ii) Since $\dfrac{1}{x-1}$ is not defined when $x = 1$, the point $x = 1$ is not in the domain of the function, but when x is close to 1, y is numerically large. Its sign can be found by saying that if x is greater than 1, $x - 1$ is positive, and if x is less than 1, $x - 1$ is negative.

(iii) The information gained so far is shown in figure 16.9(i), and it is easy to complete the sketch as shown in figure 16.9(ii). Confirmation is gained by noting that the graph does not cross the x-axis, since $\dfrac{1}{x-1} = 0$ does not have solutions.

The teacher will notice that graph-sketching from clues such as those obtained here also relies implicitly on knowledge of the continuity of the functions sketched. Many pupils are not bold enough with sketching graphs at this age. They tend to plot more points than they need and to be frightened to look for clues in the

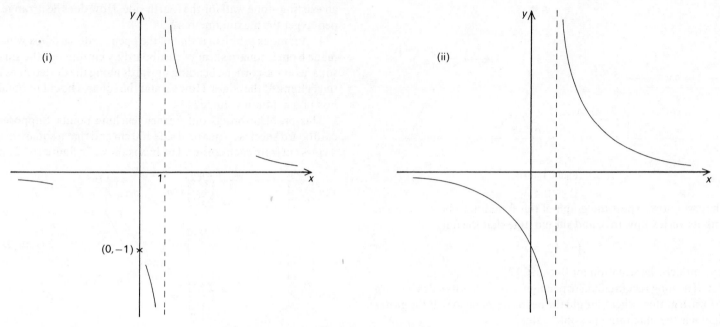

Figure 16.9 Sketch of the graph of $f: x \mapsto 1/(x-1)$.

form of the equation and in the form of the derivative (if they can calculate it).

16.3. Design Problems

Some of the most compelling and dramatic glimpses of the power of calculus come, for 16-year-old pupils, when they see how differentiation can solve problems of design.

There are many simple beautiful examples, some of which are discussed below. Pupils may well have met and solved some of these problems by careful graph-drawing earlier. Now, instead, they can sketch the graph and find the important points, which are usually points of zero gradient, by exact calculation.

1. How should a loop of string of length 24 cm be arranged on a peg-board to enclose a rectangle of maximum area? This problem will have been familiar to many pupils since their primary-school days. They can now solve it by calculation, by finding the point of zero gradient on the graph of

$$A = x(12-x)$$
$$= 12x - x^2.$$

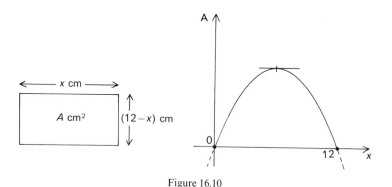

Figure 16.10

They will now expect the graph of this function to be a parabola, with its vertex upwards, and should note that the function

$$A = 12x - x^2$$

only models the situation for $0 \leqslant x \leqslant 12$.

2. The long rectangular strip in figure 16.11 has its sides bent up to form a gutter; where should the bends be made so that the gutter channels the maximum possible water?

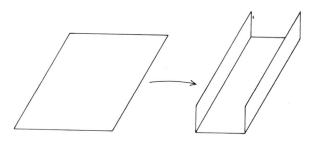

Figure 16.11

3. The farmer has a fixed length of fencing and he wishes to make a rectangular sheep pen using his fencing for three sides and an existing stone wall for the fourth side. How does he arrange the pen to get the maximum area?

4. A famous problem is that of the open cardboard box which is made from a square sheet of cardboard by cutting out the shaded squares at the corners, bending upwards along the dotted lines and then gluing at the edges. How should the squares be cut to obtain a box of maximum volume?

This problem brings out further teaching points. Suppose the cardboard sheet is a square of side 100 cm and that a square of side x cm is cut from each corner. The box is shown in figure 16.12 and it

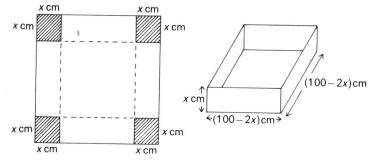

Figure 16.12

is clear that its volume, y cm^3, is given by the function

$$y = x(100 - 2x)^2 = 10\,000x - 400x^2 + 4x^3.$$

The equation models the situation only for $0 \leqslant x \leqslant 50$, and pupils should be explicitly aware of this, for it helps them to visualize the graph of the function. Clearly, the volume of the box is zero if $x = 0$ or $x = 50$. It seems as if the graph will be rather like that of figure 16.13(i). However, the function is a cubic, and figure 16.13(i) gives a poor idea of what actually happens. Moreover, pupils may expect the maximum to occur when $x = 25$.

The gradient at $x = a$ is $f'(a) = 10\,000 - 800a + 12a^2$, and this is

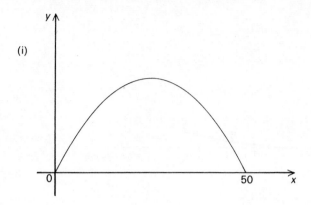

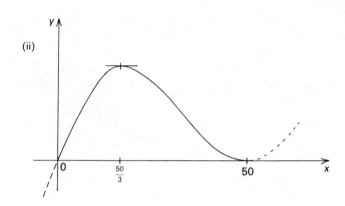

Figure 16.13

zero when $a = \frac{50}{3}$ and $a = 50$. Thus the graph is that shown in figure 16.13(ii), where the parts of the graph which do not model the physical situation are shown by dotted lines.

The box has a maximum volume of about $0·07\,\text{m}^3$; the base of this box is a square of side about 67 cm, and its height is about 17 cm: a surprising shape to give the maximum volume.

This kind of argument based on curve sketching and common sense is all that is necessary for design problems at this level. Rules to distinguish maxima from minima are not yet needed, and should not yet be introduced. For instance, in the problems just given, it is surely unnecessary to verify that $x = \frac{50}{3}$ gives a local maximum and $x = 50$ gives a local minimum for it is quite clear that when $x = 50$, the volume of the box is zero.

16.4. Step-by-Step Integration; Orienteering

Many situations exist in real life which lead to mathematical models in which the gradient of a function is known at each point,

and it is required to find the general form of the graph of the function. One example of this, which has already been examined from a different viewpoint in section 6.6, is growth; a situation in which at each instant the amount of material present increases at a rate proportional to the total amount of material there at that instant, that is, the rate of change of material is proportional to the total amount of material. This gives rise to the equation

$$f'(t) = \lambda f(t).$$

For example, the birthrate is given as 13 live births per 1000 of population, and the interest rate for investment of money is given as a percentage of the amount invested.

It is useful and constructive, both for future work and for a proper understanding of gradient, for pupils to study a step-by-step approach for finding such approximations to graphs whose gradients are known at each point.

The method is illustrated by the following example which is not related to growth. A graph passes through the point $(0,0)$ and has the property that its gradient at each point is equal to the x-

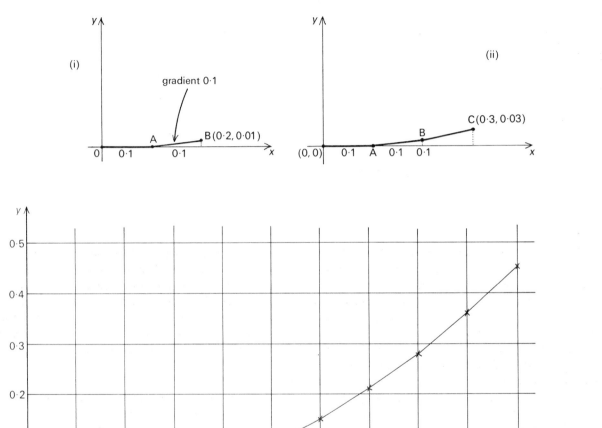

Figure 16.14   Step-by-step solution of the equation $f'(x) = x$.

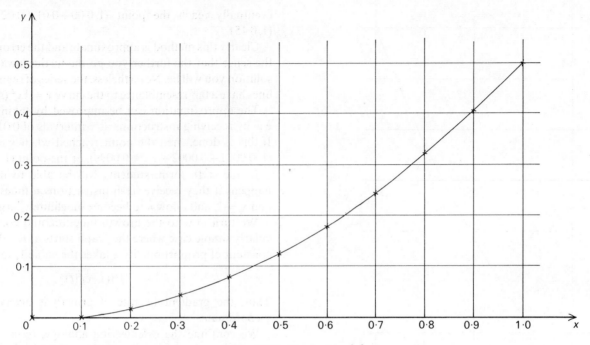

Figure 16.15   Graph of $y = \frac{1}{2}x^2$.

coordinate at that point. An approximation to the shape of this graph can be stepped out by using an idea from orienteering.

Imagine you are orienteering, that you are at $(0,0)$, and that you must walk in the direction given by a first set of instructions, and keep walking in that direction until you receive another instruction. At $(0,0)$ the x-coordinate is 0, so the gradient is 0, and the instructions are to walk along a line with gradient 0 in the direction of the positive x-axis.

The next instruction may come after walking a distance 0·1 km or on reaching the line $x = 0·1$ or according to some other rule. Suppose the next instruction is given when the point $(0·1, 0)$ is

reached. What instruction should it be? Since the gradient at that point is known to be the same as its x-coordinate, the instruction is to proceed with a gradient of 0·1 until further orders. These will be given on reaching the point with x-coordinate 0·2; that is, at B. The step in the y-direction from A to B is 0·01, so B has coordinate $(0·2, 0·01)$.

The new instruction will be to travel with gradient 0·2 until reaching a point C with x-coordinate 0·3. The step in the y-direction from B to C is 0·02, so C has coordinates $(0·3, 0·03)$. Pupils can proceed in this way using a mixture of drawing on graph paper with a large scale and calculation until they see that they

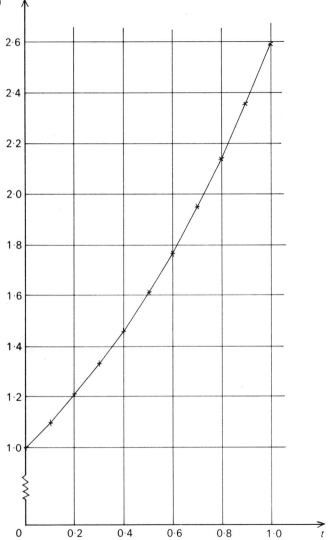

Figure 16.16   Step-by-step solution of the equation $f'(t) = f(t)$.

eventually reach the point $(1, 0{\cdot}00 + 0{\cdot}01 + 0{\cdot}02 + \ldots + 0{\cdot}09)$ or $(1, 0{\cdot}45)$.

Clearly this method is approximate and the errors will "grow" in the sense that the further you go the further away from the true solution you will be. Nevertheless, the series of segments of straight lines have a fair resemblance to the curve $y = \frac{1}{2}x^2$ (see figure 16.15).

The approximation can be improved by taking shorter steps, e.g. by receiving instructions at x-intervals of $0{\cdot}01$ instead of $0{\cdot}1$. If this is done, then the point reached when $x = 1$ is the point $(1, 0{\cdot}0001 + 0{\cdot}0002 + \ldots + 0{\cdot}0099)$, or the point $(1, 0{\cdot}495)$.

In the sixth form, students will be able to investigate what happens if they receive fresh instructions n times between $x = 0$ and $x = 1$, and allow n to become indefinitely large.

We turn now to the growth function, and consider the particularly simple case where the graph starts at $t = 0$, $y = 1$, and the constant of proportionality λ takes the value 1, so that

$$f'(t) = f(t).$$

Thus, the gradient or rate of growth is always equal to the y-coordinate.

We continue the orienteering analogy, receiving instructions whenever we have moved a distance of $0{\cdot}1$ in the t-direction. The first point reached is $A(0{\cdot}1, 1{\cdot}1)$ and the fresh instruction is to proceed with gradient $1{\cdot}1$. This leads to $B(0{\cdot}2, 1{\cdot}21)$ and the instruction to proceed with gradient $1{\cdot}21$. Working to two decimal places, which is all that can be expected using a graphical method, we eventually reach the point $(1{\cdot}0, 2{\cdot}59)$ and the y-coordinate is beginning to increase in value for each step quite quickly.

Pupils will see that the values they obtain at each point are $(0, 1)$, $(0{\cdot}1, 1{\cdot}1)$, $(0{\cdot}2, 1{\cdot}1^2), \ldots, (0{\cdot}9, 1{\cdot}1^9)$ $(1{\cdot}0, 1{\cdot}1^{10})$. The calculator shows that $1{\cdot}1^{10}$ is approximately $2{\cdot}59$. They might guess that with steps of $0{\cdot}01$, the value at $x = 1$ would be $(1{\cdot}01)^{100} \approx 2{\cdot}70$.

This method of step-by-step solution of differential equations is a very general one, and adaptations of it are used when computers are available and the equation of the curve cannot be evaluated directly. For the pupils we are considering, the beauty of the method lies first in its simplicity, and secondly in that it concentrates the pupils' attention on the meaning of gradient.

16.5. Volumes of Revolution

Many pupils are told, on the basis of very little evidence, that the volume of a circular cone is $\frac{1}{3}\pi r^2 h$, or one-third of the volume of a cylinder of the same height and radius.

For pupils who have studied the definite integral, the volume of a cone may be taken as the first example of the volume of a solid of revolution. The line through the origin with gradient $\dfrac{r}{h}$ is rotated round this x-axis, and sweeps out a circular cone of radius r and height h (figure 16.17(ii)).

This section concentrates on establishing that when the graph of $y = f(x)$ shown in figure 16.18 is rotated around the x-axis the volume of revolution generated is given by

$$\int_a^b \pi y^2 \, dx \quad \text{or} \quad \int_a^b \pi \{f(x)\}^2 \, dx.$$

The method used is to recognize that the volume of revolution generated between $x = a$ and $x = b$ is equal to the area under the graph of $y = \pi \{f(x)\}^2$ between $x = a$ and $x = b$.

The x-axis between $x = a$ and $x = b$ is divided into n equal parts each of width w. Each part gives rise to a disc with a curved surface, and a set of inner and outer cylindrical discs is constructed so that a sandwich argument can be used (figure 16.19). We see that the rotation of each strip in figure 16.19 gives

volume of inner disc $\leqslant$ volume of revolution $\leqslant$ volume of outer disc.

An enlarged view of one of these elements with its inner and

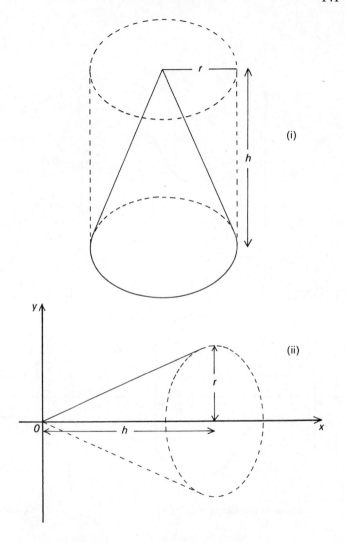

Figure 16.17   The volume of a circular cone.

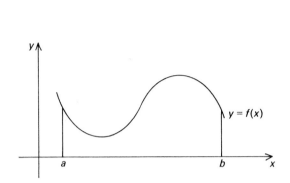

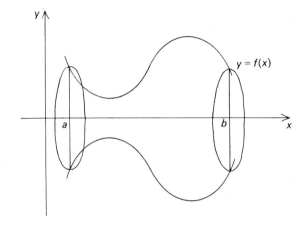

Figure 16.18

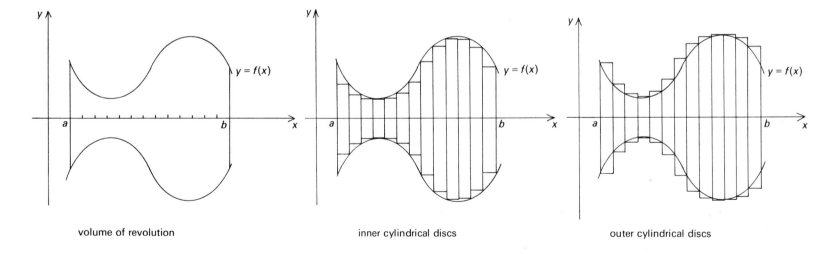

volume of revolution   inner cylindrical discs   outer cylindrical discs

Figure 16.19   Volume of revolution by a sandwiching method.

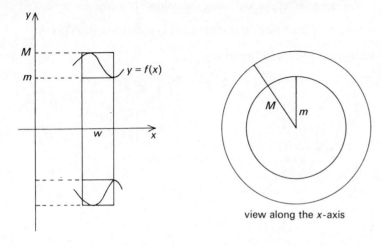

Figure 16.20

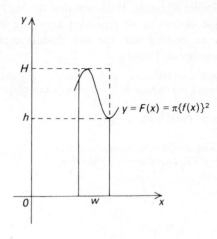

Figure 16.21

outer cylindrical discs is shown in figure 16.20. The thickness of each disc is w, while the radii of the inner and outer cylindrical discs are m and M respectively. Hence

$$\pi m^2 w \leqslant \text{volume of revolution of } y = f(x) \leqslant \pi M^2 w.$$

But this can be interpreted differently. We consider the curve $y = F(x)$ where $F(x) = \pi\{f(x)\}^2$ and calculate the area under $y = F(x)$ between $x = a$ and $x = b$. Dividing the interval between $x = a$ and $x = b$ into n equal parts as before, we can set up a correspondence between a strip of the area under $y = F(x)$ (figure 16.21) and the disc of the volume of revolution of $y = f(x)$ shown in figure 16.20. If the greatest and the least heights are H and h respectively, the sandwich inequality for area is

$$hw \leqslant \text{area under } y = F(x) \leqslant Hw.$$

But $h = \pi m^2$ and $H = \pi M^2$, since $F(x) = \pi\{f(x)\}^2$. Thus

$$hw \leqslant \text{volume of revolution of } y = f(x) \leqslant Hw.$$

Now we can compare two sandwich inequalities

$hw =$ lower step-function area for $F(x)$	$\leqslant$ volume of revolution of $\leqslant$ $y = f(x)$ $\leqslant$ area under $y = F(x)$ $\leqslant$	$Hw =$ upper step-function area for $F(x)$

and add the similar inequalities for all the discs between $x = a$ and $x = b$. When this is done we reach the inequality

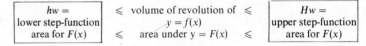

This is a familiar situation. We know that the sandwich inequality can be made as thin as we please by choosing w small enough. From this we deduce that the two middle expressions in the sandwich are equal. Thus

$$\text{volume of solid of revolution of } y = f(x) \text{ between } x = a \text{ and } x = b = \text{area under } y = F(x) \text{ between } x = a \text{ and } x = b = \int_a^b F(x)dx.$$

But $F(x) = \pi\{f(x)\}^2$, so

$$\text{volume of solid of revolution generated by } y = f(x) \text{ between } x = a \text{ and } x = b = \int_a^b \pi\{f(x)\}^2 \, dx.$$

We can now return to finding the volume of a circular cone. The equation of the function whose graph is rotated is $y = f(x) = \dfrac{r}{h}x.$

Hence the volume of the cone is

$$\int_0^h \pi\left\{\frac{r}{h}x\right\}^2 dx = \frac{\pi r^2}{h^2}\int_0^h x^2 \, dx$$

$$= \frac{\pi r^2}{h^2}\left[\frac{x^3}{3}\right]_0^h$$

$$= \tfrac{1}{3}\pi r^2 h.$$

17 The Early Historical Development of Calculus R.L.E.Schwarzenberger

The teaching of differentiation and integration in Britain has suffered through an unfortunate historical accident. Patriotic pride in the achievements of Newton, ignorance of continental developments, and distrust of pure mathematics all contributed to a view of "the Calculus" as an isolated, awe-inspiring, impossibly difficult and almost magical event.

The material in this book makes it clear that, on the contrary, differentiation and integration arose in a context of other work and to serve particular purposes. This is also apparent from the very explicit titles of the monographs of Newton himself: *On Analysis by means of Equations with an Infinite Number of Terms*[1], *Methods of Fluxions and Infinite Series*[2], *On Quadrature of Curves*[3]. On the Continent the successors of Leibniz improved and simplified the subject: it became more common to use ordinary words (for example *Differentialrechnung* and *calcul différentiel* meaning differentiation, *Integralrechnung* and *calcul intégral* meaning integration) of the same kind as the words used to describe other methods of calculation, which had the further advantage of making clear that differentiation and integration are different methods which came about in different ways and for different purposes.

It is therefore particularly necessary in Britain to teach differentiation and integration within a context in which they arise naturally, and not as an isolated abstruse phenomenon with a mystical Latin title. The range of current applications of differentiation and integration gives a clear indication that the most helpful *mathematical* context is that of graphs and functions adopted in this book. The *historical* context is closely related, but leads to slightly different insights. It clarifies the physical problems from which the ideas of differentiation and integration arose, and so may give a guide to possible topics for use as examples or as motivation in the classroom today. It makes clear that integration arose from much simpler problems than differentiation, and at a very much earlier date, and so raises the question whether integration is not more "natural" and more suitable for teaching at an early stage. It shows the enormous conceptual simplification and unification which came about through the systematic use of coordinates and graphs: a good example of the way in which mathematics progresses by taking advantage of simpler notation, as well as by creating new theories.

17.1. The Origins of Graphical Methods

The modern habit of plotting graphs is so familiar that it is now hard to realize that it is relatively recent. The plotting of data by chemists and physicists, whether as a smooth curve or by isolated values or by block graphs, is difficult to trace back beyond the eighteenth century.

The solution of geometrical problems by the use of algebraic equations involving coordinates dates from Descartes[4] and Fermat[5] in the early seventeenth century: to the extent that the systematic use of coordinates is the essential feature of modern graphical work, they must be credited with its discovery.

---

[1] *De Analysi per Aequationes Numero Terminorum Infinitas*, 1711 (written *c.* 1669).

[2] *Methodus Fluxionum et Serierum Infinitarum*, 1736 (written *c.* 1671).

[3] *De Quadratura Curvarum*, 1704 (written *c.* 1676).

[4] *La Géométrie*, 1637.

[5] *Ad Locos Planos et Solidos Isagoge*, 1679 (written *c.* 1629).

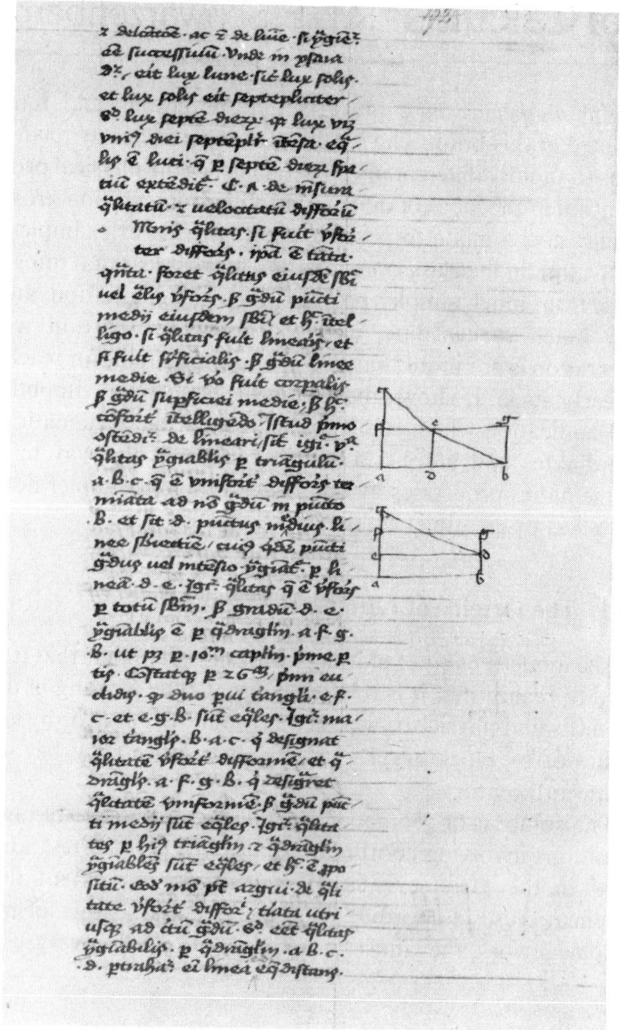

Figure 17.1 Graphs in a manuscript of Oresme of 1428 (British Library, Sloane, MS 2156). The graphs represent a "quality" (given by height above the "subject line" *ab*) which is decreasing steadily. The "uniform quality", or constant, which has the same area under the graph, is given by the horizontal line *fg*.

But the representation of quantities by lengths and areas on geometrical diagrams has a longer history. In the fourteenth century, Nicole Oresme[6] represented time and velocity by lengths, and distance travelled by area, on diagrams not dissimilar from those in chapter 11. In the eleventh century, Omar Khayyam[7]—better known today for his collection of light verse—used intersecting conics to construct a length representing the root of a cubic equation. Both Oresme and Khayyam were not merely mathematicians: they made contributions to economics and to astronomy respectively. Similarly the writings of the Greek geometers on astronomy, geography, mechanics and optics show clearly that for them geometry was closely linked to physical applications: the length and area of a geometrical diagram could be used to represent physical quantities.

Here, even if coordinates are not used systematically, is the origin of modern graphical work and also the origin of calculus. Its development can be seen most clearly in the work of the Greek geometers on area, and in the problems studied by the Pythagorean school 2500 years ago.

17.2. Pythagoras

The study of area under the Pythagorean school followed the method familiar in primary schools of dissecting a region into parts and reassembling them to form a known area. The rules for doing

---

[6] *De Uniformitate et Difformitate Intensionum, c.* 1350.

[7] *Algebra, c.* 1080.

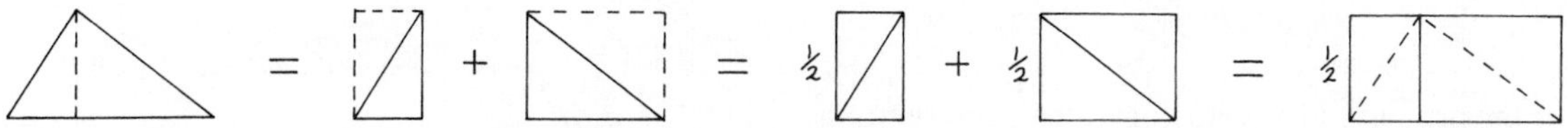

Figure 17.2

so were expressed in "axioms" such as "if equals be added to equals, the wholes are equal" and "the whole is greater than the parts". Once the area of rectangles is taken for granted, other areas can be determined without further assumptions. For example, the dissection shown in figure 17.2 gives the area of a triangle as $\frac{1}{2}$ base × height, and in fact yields three equivalent expressions for this area (taking different sides as base). The consequences of this equivalence are non-trivial. For example, it is a short step to the fact (equivalent to Pythagoras' theorem) that, if ABC is a right-angled triangle, then the two areas shaded in figure 17.3 (where AB = AD and AC = AE) are equal.

The procedure, of deducing non-trivial results about area from very elementary assumptions, is precisely that used in "measure theory" today. If these methods are combined with the notion of similar triangles, there are further consequences. For example, if r is the radius (distance from centre to any vertex) of a regular polygon with N sides then the length s of each edge, and the distance t from the centre to the mid-point of each edge, are each proportional to r by the properties of similar triangles. It follows that the area of a regular polygon with N sides is proportional to the square of its radius.

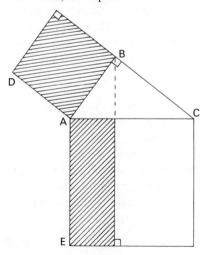

Figure 17.3

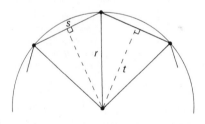

Figure 17.4

The most significant steps towards the calculus, from such elementary calculations, were those attributed by later Greek mathematicians to Eudoxus. It is tragic that no edition of his work survives, but it is possible to guess much of the content from the description given by Euclid.

17.3. Eudoxus

It is sufficient for the present purpose to illustrate the power and precision of Eudoxus by explaining in modern notation one particular theorem: the fact that a circle of radius r has area proportional to r^2. This theorem also illustrates the way in which the successive attempts by mathematicians from Euclid onwards to make the results of Eudoxus understandable to the reader have done so at the price of introducing vague concepts which have harmed mathematical education ever since, and which are still used by many teachers at all levels. It would, for example, be asserted that "Polygons inscrib'd in a Circle infinitely at last end in the Circle", and hence that the area of a circle is proportional to the square of the radius by an immediate deduction from the corresponding fact already established for polygons. The assertion and the deduction are a common feature of editions of Euclid, but neither makes much sense to the thoughtful pupil: both fully deserve the denunciation made by Berkeley[8] when he asked

> Whether men may properly be said to proceed in a scientific method, without clearly conceiving the object they are conversant about, the end proposed, and the method by which it is pursued?... Whether the same things which are now done by infinities may not be done by finite quantities? And whether this would not be a great relief to the imaginations and understanding of mathematical men?

None of these criticisms apply to Eudoxus who was, as far as one can tell, careful to avoid the notions of "infinite", "approximation" and "exhaustion" which later less-clear-thinking generations adopted. His work depends on the relationship between the areas A, A_N and A_{2N} of the circle, N-sided polygon and $2N$-sided

[8] *The Analyst*, or *A Discourse Addressed to an Infidel Mathematician.* Wherein it is examined whether the Object, Principles, and Inferences of the Modern Analysis are more distinctly conceived, or more evidently deduced, than Religious Mysteries and Points of Faith. "First cast out the beam out of thine own Eye; and then shalt thou see clearly to cast out the mote out of they brother's Eye", 1734.

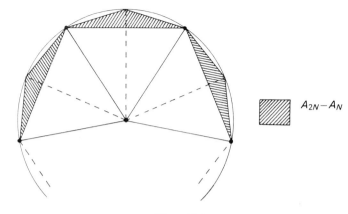

$$A_{2N} - A_N$$

Figure 17.5

polygon for a given value of N. Thus $A_{2N} - A_N$ is the area of the additional triangles needed to form a regular polygon with $2N$ sides from a regular polygon with N sides, while $A - A_{2N}$ is the area of the segments of the circle which remain outside the larger polygon. A dissection (figure 17.6) shows that

$$A - A_{2N} < \tfrac{1}{2}(A - A_N),$$

since each side of the inequality can be represented by the sum of N regions (one for each side of the polygon) of the kind shaded in figure 17.6. Thus the area left outside the polygon is more than halved each time the number of sides is doubled (to see this in practice work out the areas of polygons with 4, 8, 16, ... etc., sides using a calculator with a square root—no trigonometry is needed). But the heart of Eudoxus' method is not in proceeding to alleged limits; it is in the more straightforward theorem which states that

If $B < A$ there is an integer N such that $B < A_N$:

In more colloquial language, given any area B less than that of the

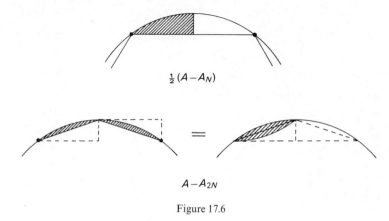

$$\tfrac{1}{2}(A - A_N)$$

$$A - A_{2N}$$

Figure 17.6

circle, there are inscribed regular polygons with area larger than B. It is this theorem which can now be used to prove that the area of a circle is proportional to the square of its radius.

The argument is as follows. Recall that we already know the result for a regular polygon with N sides, so that if two circles have areas A, A' and radii r, r', then the areas of the corresponding polygons satisfy

$$k^2 A'_N = A_N$$

where k is the ratio r/r'. Now compare $k^2 A'$ with A. If $k^2 A' < A$, then by the theorem established above there is an integer N such that $k^2 A' < A_N$; but this implies $k^2 A' < k^2 A'_N$ in contradiction to the fact that $A'_N < A'$. Again, if $A < k^2 A'$ there is an integer N such that $A < k^2 A'_N$ because the same theorem can be applied to the circle of radius r'; but this implies $A < A_N$ in contradiction to the fact that $A_N < A$. Since both $k^2 A' < A$ and $A < k^2 A'$ are false, the only possibility remaining is the equality $k^2 A' = A$ which was to be proved.

Notice the completely rigorous nature of this proof, and also the absence of spurious appeals to "infinites" or "approximations".

The same combination of rigour and straightforwardness can be seen even more clearly in the subsequent work of Archimedes, since his own commentary on the method has survived.

17.4. Archimedes

A good example of the work of Archimedes is his determination of the area of the segment of a parabola. In the diagram, the segment in question is bounded by the chord RS and T is the point

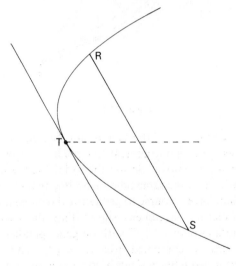

Figure 17.7

with tangent parallel to RS. The problem is to relate the area A of the segment to the area A_0 of the triangle RST. Archimedes proves that $A = \tfrac{4}{3} A_0$ in the following four stages.

(i) A centre-of-gravity argument applied to strips parallel to the axis of the parabola suggests $\tfrac{4}{3} A_0$ as a likely guess for the value of A.

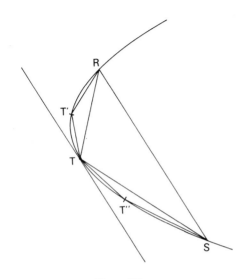

Figure 17.8

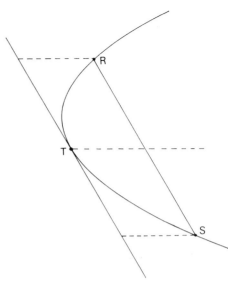

Figure 17.9

Archimedes' comment is "the fact is not demonstrated by the argument used; but that argument has given a sort of indication that the conclusion is true. Seeing then that the theorem is not demonstrated, but at the same time suspecting that the conclusion is true, we shall have recourse to geometrical demonstration ...".

(ii) A geometrical argument shows that the two triangles formed by adding points T', T'' with tangents parallel to RT, ST respectively have a combined area $A_1 = \frac{1}{4}A_0$. The same construction performed n times yields a polygon with area

$$A_0 + A_1 + \ldots + A_n = A_0 + \frac{1}{4}A_0 + \ldots + \frac{1}{4^n}A_0.$$

But $\left(1 + \frac{1}{4} + \ldots + \frac{1}{4^n}\right)\left(1 - \frac{1}{4}\right) = 1 - \frac{1}{4} \times \frac{1}{4^n}$ and therefore the polygon has area $\frac{4}{3}A_0 - \frac{1}{3}A_n$.

(iii) Comparing the area A with that of the parallelogram with side RS we see that $A_0 < A < 2A_0$. The same argument applied to each stage of the preceding construction shows that

$$\tfrac{4}{3}A_0 - \tfrac{1}{3}A_n < A < \tfrac{4}{3}A_0 + \tfrac{2}{3}A_n.$$

(iv) Since $A_n = \frac{1}{4^n} A_0$ is obtained by successive quartering, it is true that if $\frac{4}{3}A_0 < A$ there is a value of n for which $\frac{4}{3}A_0 + \frac{2}{3}A_n < A$, while if $A < \frac{4}{3}A_0$ there is a value of n for which $A < \frac{4}{3}A_0 - \frac{1}{3}A_n$. Either case contradicts the inequality obtained above; the only possibility remaining is the equality $\frac{4}{3}A_0 = A$ which was to be proved.

This argument is that of Archimedes subject only to the use of modern notation. The four stages are typical of the method used in many other problems:

(i) to guess the answer, often by the use of physical argument;

(ii) to establish a geometrical result which ensures that a known area or volume can be built up from blocks of diminishing size;

(iii) to prove that the required area or volume is bounded above and below by known areas or volume;

(iv) to show that the area or volume is neither more nor less than that guessed initially.

The great merit of the method is the absence of "infinites" and "approximations". Its great defect is that each problem must be attacked separately and may require ingenious geometrical arguments. When Greek mathematics began once again to be studied and understood in the fourteenth, fifteenth and sixteenth centuries, the stumbling block to further progress was the lack of any general method which would be applicable to a wide range of problems and which would contain as special cases the results of Eudoxus and Archimedes. The discovery of such a method had to await the systematic use of coordinates in graphical work due to Descartes and, when it came, the method lacked the straightforward precision characteristic of Eudoxus and Archimedes.

17.5. The Early Seventeenth Century

The turmoil of the first half of the seventeenth century was characterized in mathematics by much speculation on problems arising from graphical work and from physical applications: the correct definition of the tangent to a curve at a given point, of maxima and minima of given functions, of the length of a curve, of the relationship between velocity and distance, and so on. But initially the most substantial progress was made on questions concerning area and volumes. There are two natural reasons for this: there was no problem of finding correct definitions, since results on area depend only on very simple axioms and not on the

particular definitions, and moreover the methods of Eudoxus and Archimedes were available and could easily be adapted to the new coordinate geometry.

Three examples must suffice; all are not merely of historical interest but could also provide teaching material for pupils at the corresponding stage of development. The first is the work of Cavalieri[9] on the area under the curve $y = x^p$. In modern notation his result would be written

$$\int_0^a x^p \, dx = \frac{1}{p+1} a^{p+1}$$

but in fact he appears first to have noted that the integral is proportional to a^{p+1}. Today we would prove this fact using the method of substitution: if $a' = ta$ then

$$\int_0^{a'} x^p \, dx = \int_0^{ta} x^p \, dx = \int_0^a (ty)^p t \, dy$$

where $x = ty$. Thus

$$\int_0^{a'} x^p \, dx = t^{p+1} \int_0^a y^p \, dy$$

and therefore, writing $I(a)$ for $\int_0^a x^p \, dx$, we obtain the required "homogeneity property"

$$I(a') = t^{p+1} I(a).$$

However, this fact can be understood in a more elementary fashion. If the region between $x = 0$ and $x = a$ is cut into strips of width w, then the region between $x = 0$ and $x = ta$ can be cut into the same number of strips of width tw (figure 17.10). The height of each strip is now multiplied by a factor t^p. The required result is now immediately plausible. The method of Eudoxus would then

---

[9] *Centuria de Varii Problemii*, 1639.

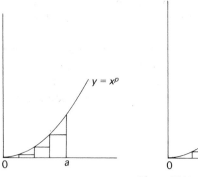
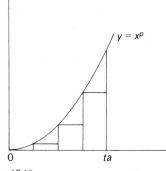

Figure 17.10

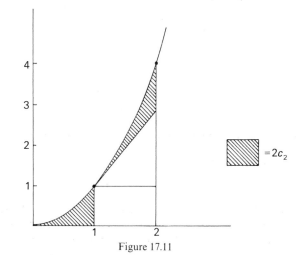

$= 2c_2$

Figure 17.11

and confusing notion of "indivisibles". Once it is known that the integral has the form $c_p a^{p+1}$, where c_p is a constant depending on p, then it is easy to form recurrence relations which determine c_p in terms of $c_1, c_2, \ldots, c_{p-1}$. The pupil who is asked to do this will learn a lot in the process, but should be told that Cavalieri himself only got up to $p = 9$.

Example: To find c_2 knowing $c_1 = \frac{1}{2}$. The homogeneity argument implies

$$8c_2 = 8\int_0^1 x^2\,dx = \int_0^2 x^2\,dx = \int_0^1 x^2\,dx + \int_1^2 x^2\,dx = c_2 + \int_0^1 (x+1)^2\,dx$$

But $\int_0^1 (x+1)^2\,dx = c_2 + 2c_1 + 1 = c_2 + 2$. Therefore $8c_2 = c_2 + c_2 + 2$. We conclude that $c_2 = \frac{1}{3}$ (see figure 17.11).

The second example is the work of Fermat[10] on the same problem. Essentially he used steps of width w where $a = Nw$ obtaining the inequality

$$w(1^p w^p + \ldots + (N-1)^p w^p) < \int_0^a x^p\,dx < w(w^p + 2^p w^p + \ldots + N^p w^p)$$

$$\frac{a^{p+1}}{N^{p+1}}(1^p + \ldots + (N-1)^p) < \int_0^a x^p\,dx < \frac{a^{p+1}}{N^{p+1}}(1^p + 2^p + \ldots + N^p).$$

This is an efficient "sandwich" if, but only if, there is available an algebraic formula for the sum $1^p + 2^p + \ldots + N^p$ in terms of N.

Example: The case $p = 2$. The formula $\frac{1}{6}N(N+1)(2N+1)$ for the sum of the first N squares implies

$$\frac{a^3}{6N^3}(N-1)N(2N-1) < \int_0^a x^2\,dx < \frac{a^3}{6N^3}N(N+1)(2N+1)$$

$$\frac{a^3}{3} - \frac{a^3}{2N} + \frac{a^3}{6N^2} < \int_0^a x^2\,dx < \frac{a^3}{3} + \frac{a^3}{2N} + \frac{a^3}{6N^2}$$

and it is easy to see that the integral can be neither more or less than $\frac{1}{3}a^3$.

serve to establish it rigorously, as would the "sandwich" method which can be found in chapter 13, but Cavalieri appears not to have argued in this way: instead he introduced the unfortunate

---

[10] *Varia Opera Mathematica*, 1679 (written c. 1630).

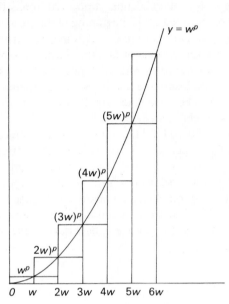

Figure 17.12

The third example concerns the area under the graph $y = \dfrac{1}{x}$ and is attributed to Gregory of St. Vincent[11]. The same homogeneity argument, used by Cavalieri for other powers of x, implies

$$\int_1^{ab} \frac{1}{x}\,dx = \int_1^a \frac{1}{x}\,dx + \int_a^{ab} \frac{1}{x}\,dx = \int_1^a \frac{1}{x}\,dx + \int_1^b \frac{1}{x}\,dx.$$

As Gregory's pupil Sarasa[12] observed in his own work, the areas behave like logarithms. Even today, this is probably the most satisfactory way to introduce natural logarithms.

---

[11] *Opus Geometricum Quadratura Circuli et Sectionum Coni*, 1647.

[12] *Solutio Problematis a Mersenno Propositi*, 1649.

It is significant that in all these examples it is not necessary to know anything about area beyond the axioms used by the Greeks. The results can all be established by the method of Eudoxus, that is to say without introducing "infinites", "approximations" or (a term which made its appearance in the work of Gregory of St. Vincent) "exhaustion". However, it was by the use of such language that mathematicians searched for a general method which would reduce the calculation of areas to a more mechanical and less ingenious process.

17.6. Newton and Leibniz

The long-sought general method came from an unexpected quarter. It was not an algorithm for integration, but a highly efficient machine for doing the opposite. It was undoubtedly the study of velocity-time graphs which led Newton to the realization that the ordinates of a graph give a direct measure of the rate of change, or gradient, of the area under the graph. His results on this question yielded a general method for determining gradients. Once the basic properties of differentiation had been established, it became evident that Newton and Leibniz had created a tool which was astonishingly easy to use. The derivatives of all kinds of functions could be obtained by a unified method; whenever, by chance, there appeared among the list of derivatives a known function, then areas under the graph of the latter function could be determined.

With the use of coordinates it became evident that much of the work of Eudoxus and Archimedes consisted of different instances of the integration of functions like $x \mapsto x$ and $x \mapsto x^2$, and that this itself was merely the consequence of the differentiation of functions like $x \mapsto x^2$ and $x \mapsto x^3$. The way was open to the calculation of more complicated areas and volumes, to an understanding of the length of curves and the calculus of variations and to the solution of differential equations.

With hindsight we can see that the achievement of Newton and Leibniz was built upon a vast body of results established by the mathematicians of the early seventeenth century: not merely those mentioned above by way of example but also such men as Kepler, Roberval, Wallis, Barrow and Gregory. On the other hand, the dramatic power of the technique of differentiation, and the extreme difficulty which was experienced in justifying and in explaining the concepts and techniques involved in its creation, combined to set differentiation (and hence also its opposite, integration) apart as "the Calculus". The result was a tension between two extremes. On the one hand were the geometric problems from which calculus arose, especially those concerning area and volume; the concepts were clear, and could be applied to prove satisfying general results or to justify results guessed by other methods, but any *particular* numerical determination of area or volume required either an ingenious special argument or the restatement of the problem in more algebraic terms followed by recourse to results from differentiation.

On the other hand, there was the supremely efficient algebraic tool of differentiation which was very difficult to understand and which appeared mystical or even magical when attempts were made to explain how or why it worked.

So powerful was the spell cast by this algebraic tool that the origins of calculus in the calculation of areas were almost forgotten. Differentiation took over from integration, and mathematicians, instead of viewing differentiation as a method for finding gradients, began to view it as the subject matter of calculus *par excellence*.

They even began to introduce a so-called "indefinite integration" as the opposite of differentiation, so that the pupil was faced first with the concept of differentiation whose definition was most obscure, and then with two sorts of integration, indefinite and

definite. Inevitably "the Calculus" appeared impossibly abstruse and the harm described at the beginning of this essay was done. It was only by a gradual return to more geometrical methods, and by a rejection of infinitesimals in favour of a more sensible understanding of real numbers and of limits, that the balance was gradually restored and the methods of differentiation and integration could take their place among the ordinary concepts of mathematics taught at an elementary level.

At a more advanced level the return to more geometric methods has provided a proper basis for the calculus of functions of several variables. Integration, partial differentiation and calculus of variations all now arise from a fusion of the analytic methods of calculus and the geometric methods of linear algebra. The right balance must be achieved between algebraic manipulations and geometric concepts, for both are necessary if the subject is to progress healthily.

17.7. Conclusions

What conclusions does the historical development of calculus suggest for the teacher of graphical work today? Those who believe that historical development is a good guide to psychological development in individuals might find it useful to chart the former in terms of the dichotomy between "relational" and "instrumental" understanding popularized by Skemp[13]. The sum total of man's knowledge of calculus might be displayed as a trail traced on a diagram, in which fast progress was made in the three periods 400–200 BC, AD 1600–1700, AD 1850–1950 and very slow progress in the periods between. Perhaps there is a case for building up the knowledge of the individual pupil by much the same route? If so, three conclusions suggest themselves.

Firstly, calculus has its roots in geometrical problems so that it is

---

[13] *The Psychology of Learning Mathematics*, Pelican 1971.

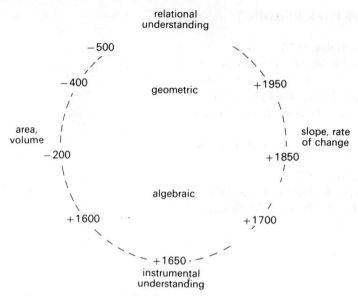

Figure 17.13   Historical development of man's knowledge of calculus.

essential for good understanding to use geometric diagrams and not merely to rely on algebraic symbols.

Secondly, the concepts associated with calculus are an essential part of graphical work and may be expected to enter at an early stage. The first such concepts are likely to arise from the estimation of area and volume, and these will be accepted naturally by quite young pupils. Area is important both for its own sake and to calculate other quantities.

Thirdly, understanding of gradients and derivatives is likely to be achieved only by pupils at age fifteen or sixteen. Perhaps this is because ratio is a much more sophisticated concept than area. It suggests that differentiation should be deferred until after integration. It should arise in the first instance as a set of rules for calculation of gradients which turns out, surprisingly, to be a successful aid for evaluating definite integrals. One advantage of this approach is that it stresses that differentiation is an exact process rather than some kind of approximation.

If these conclusions suggested by the history of the development of calculus were to be adopted, pupils would see calculus as a natural development of the ideas of area and gradient. They would have seen successive stages of the function of the concepts of area and gradient, through quantitative pictorial ideas to exact calculations, and would be led by this route to a greater understanding of calculus.

SUGGESTIONS FOR FURTHER READING

1. Apostal, T. M., *Calculus I and II*, Wiley, 1976.
2. Flegg, G. and Meetham, R. (editors), *An Introduction to Calculus and Algebra—Volume I: Background to Calculus, Volume II: Calculus Applied*, Open University Press, 1971.
3. Maxwell, E. A., *Analytical Calculus, Volumes I, II, III and IV*, CUP.
4. Montgomery, R. M. N. and Jones, T. A., *Calculus and Elementary Functions*, CUP, 1970.
5. Spivak, Michael, *Calculus*, Benjamin, 1967.
6. Wheeler, David, *R is for Real*, Open University Press, 1974.
7. Williams, E. M. and Shuard, H. B., *Primary Mathematics Today*, second edition, Longman, 1976.

Index

Titles of books and journals are given in italics